Elite Voices

TRANSFORM YOUR THOUGHTS,

WHY

TAKE CONTROL OF YOUR FINANCES,

Not

AND UNLOCK LIFELONG FREEDOM

Me?

TRANSFORM YOUR THOUGHTS,

WHY

TAKE CONTROL OF YOUR FINANCES,

Not

AND UNLOCK LIFELONG FREEDOM

Me?

MANUEL RUIZ, CFP®

Elite Voices

Elite Voices
San Antonio, TX 78229

First Edition, September 2025
ISBN: 978-1-63765-837-6
Library of Congress Control Number: 2025919930

Contents

INTRODUCTION

The Distance Between Dreams and Destiny

I was ten years old when I asked my mother the question that would change everything.

We were sitting at our chipped kitchen table in Jersey City, the same table where she counted and recounted crumpled bills every month, trying to make miracles happen with mathematics. The linoleum was peeling. The radiator was hissing. My mother's shoulders carried the weight of every unpaid bill and every impossible choice between groceries and gas money.

I watched her finger tap nervously against a stack of envelopes, her calculator worn smooth from overuse. The rent notice sat unopened, but we both knew what it said.

"Mom," I said, my voice cutting through the suffocating silence, "why do we always talk about stretching what we have? Why don't we ever talk about how to make MORE?"

She looked up from the bills, and for the first time in my life, I saw something shift in her eyes. Not anger. Not dismissal. Recognition. I'd finally asked the question she'd been carrying in her heart her whole life but never dared to speak.

That moment—that crack in the foundation of everything I'd been taught about money—was the beginning of a journey that would take me from the railroad apartments of Jersey City to the gleaming towers of Wall Street. From watching my mother stretch pennies to helping families build generational wealth. From asking "Why not me?" to helping others discover their own answer to that life-changing question.

But this isn't just my story. It's yours too.

Somewhere in your life, you've felt that same suffocating weight of financial limitation. You've stood on the outside looking in, wondering why wealth and freedom seem reserved for "other people." You've asked yourself if this is all there is and if you're destined to spend your life managing scarcity but know you can create abundance instead.

I'm here to tell you that the only thing standing between you and the financial life you want is the story you've been telling yourself, not your education, your background, or your circumstances.

THE THREE QUESTIONS THAT CHANGE EVERYTHING

Every financial transformation begins with three fundamental questions that serve as a framework for everything in this book:

Why? What's your deeper purpose for building wealth? Is it creating a legacy, giving yourself freedom, or building security for the people you love? Maybe it's all three.

Why Not Now? Why are you waiting for the "perfect" moment? Or a bigger salary? Or a clearer path? Time is your most valuable asset, and every day you delay will cost you compound growth.

Why Not Me? What limiting beliefs are you carrying about who gets to build wealth? If others have broken free from financial struggle, what makes you think you can't?

These are not just philosophical questions—they are the foundation of every financial decision you will ever make. They push you to understand your motivations, recognize the urgency of action, and challenge the invisible barriers holding you back.

TRUSTING THE MESSENGER BEFORE THE MESSAGE

Before we dive into strategies and tactics, you need to know why you should listen to me when it comes to your money. Trust isn't built through credentials alone, it's earned through results and relatability.

I've managed over a hundred of million in assets as a Certified Financial Planner and founder of Compass Private Wealth. But more importantly, I've lived the transformation I'm teaching. I've lived the experience of walking the path from financial struggle to financial freedom.

I understand what it's like to grow up in a family where money conversations happen in whispers of worry, instead of declarations of possibility. I know the weight of being the first in your family to navigate investment decisions. I've felt the impostor syndrome that comes with sitting in rooms where generational wealth is the norm, not the exception. But I've also experienced the profound shift that happens when you stop accepting limitations and start creating possibilities. When you move from managing scarcity to building abundance. When you transform from someone who hopes for financial security to someone who systematically creates it.

That transformation isn't just possible for you; it will be achievable once you understand and apply the principles in this book.

THE ROADMAP TO FINANCIAL TRANSFORMATION

This book will take you on the same journey I traveled from scarcity to abundance. Along the way, you'll understand each concept and how to apply them to your own finance journeys:

Part I: Mindset - "Why Not Me?"

- How to identify and rewrite the money stories that have been unconsciously limiting your growth
- How to use psychology to transform financial fear into strategic confidence
- Why your financial identity matters more than your current income
- How to build the mental frameworks that separate wealth dreamers from wealth builders

Part II: Mechanics - "Building the Blueprint"

- The financial fundamentals every wealth builder must master
- Building a seasonal approach to investing that aligns your strategy with your life stage

- Learning the five immutable laws that govern wealth creation * *Note: (Ignore these at your peril!)*
- Determining investment metrics that separate professional wealth builders from amateur speculators
- Understanding the tax and legal strategies that protect and multiply what you've built

Part III: Legacy - "Why Not Us?"

- How to design an estate plan that transfers both wealth and wisdom
- How to create family financial systems that build generational prosperity
- The art of raising financially literate children
- How to create a financial legacy that outlives you

But more than tactics and strategies, this book is about transformation. It's about the moment you stop being a victim of your circumstances and start becoming the architect of your financial future.

THE PROOF IS IN THE PEOPLE

Over my career, I have helped ordinary people achieve extraordinary financial results through changing how they think about money and teaching them how to align their actions with abundance instead of scarcity.

There's Teresa, a single mother and teacher who couldn't look at her bank balance without anxiety. Today, she owns several rental properties and has built a substantial investment portfolio while teaching financial literacy workshops.

There's James, the postal worker who quietly built a dividend portfolio exceeding seven figures on a $65,000 salary, proving that wealth is about strategy, not income

There's the construction company owner who transformed his figure revenue into generational wealth through systematic planning, which allowed him to create financial security for the next three generations of his family.

The specifics differ, but the pattern is identical: people who seemed "ordinary" by external measures all possessed something extraordinary, the willingness to challenge their own limiting beliefs about money and take consistent action toward a bigger vision. After reading this book, you will be prepped to do the same.

WHY THIS MATTERS, ESPECIALLY NOW

We're living in unprecedented times. The economy is unpredictable. Job security is a myth. Traditional retirement planning is broken. Meanwhile, the wealth gap continues to widen, and financial literacy remains criminally undertaught.

But here's what I've learned – as the son of two immigrants and through twenty years of experience in finance: **Financial freedom isn't about external circumstances, but by internal choices.**

The same economic forces that destroy some people, can create opportunities for others. The difference isn't luck or privilege, instead it's mindset, knowledge, and the courage to act when others are paralyzed by fear.

Consider this: Strategic wealth builders see opportunities to buy quality investments at discounted prices. Right now, while many people are worried about inflation, smart investors are buying assets that historically outpace inflation. While some people complain about rising costs, entrepreneurs are creating businesses that solve these exact problems.

The external environment is the same for everyone. What differs is how you choose to respond to it.

FROM JERSEY CITY TO WALL STREET, AND BACK AGAIN

Growing up just one mile from Wall Street in Jersey City, I learned early that money wasn't just about numbers; it was about opportunity, dignity, and legacy. My parents didn't have significant wealth to pass down, but they gave me something more valuable: an unshakable belief in education, resilience, and power to control your own destiny.

They taught me that success isn't given —it's built one decision at a time.

That belief carried me from a small Jesuit prep school to Rutgers University; from working on Prudential's IPO to Ernst & Young; from Wall Street firms JP Morgan and Merrill Lynch to ultimately starting my own investment advisory firm, Compass Private Wealth.

The journey wasn't always smooth. There were moments of doubt, setbacks that felt like failures, and times when the safe path of following family expectations seemed smarter than forging my own way. But each challenge taught me something crucial about the difference between surviving and thriving, between managing money and building wealth.

But the most important lesson didn't come from any of those experiences. It came from that moment at the kitchen table when a ten-year-old boy dared to ask a different question about money: "Why not me?"

Asking "Why not me?" demands an answer that will truly change your life.

THE FEATURES THAT MAKE THIS DIFFERENT

This isn't another generic personal finance book filled with recycled advice about budgeting and cutting expenses. This is a complete system for financial transformation based on:

The Money Archetypes Framework: Discovering your financial personality and leveraging its strengths while managing its blind spots

The Four Seasons of Wealth: Learn how to align your investment strategies with your life stages for optimal results

The Wealth Builder's Dashboard: Track the metrics that matter for long-term wealth creation

The Five Laws of Wealth: Immutable principles that govern financial success

Behavioral Investment Architecture: Build portfolios based on how humans behave, not how economic models pretend they do

Legacy Design Systems: Create wealth that doesn't just survive generational transfer but grows through it

Each framework based on principles applied with real clients and informed by practical experience, rather than theoretical classroom exercises.

A GLIMPSE BEHIND THE CURTAIN

Throughout this book, you'll meet the physician who kept his money in checking accounts because her grandmother lost everything in the Depression, and you'll see how we gradually shifted her mindset from protection to strategic growth.

You'll discover how a middle school teacher built a portfolio that exceeded $2 million by never missing a monthly investment, and alternatively how high-earning executives mismanaged their wealth because they could not control their spending.

You'll learn about the family who lost his wealth in two years by panic-selling during market corrections, and the retiree who gained over $200,000 by staying calm during the same period..

These aren't cautionary tales or inspirational platitudes. They're windows into the soul of human psychology, revealing the emotional and behavioral patterns that can light your way toward abundance.

YOUR MOMENT OF CHOICE

Right now, you're standing at the same crossroads I faced at that kitchen table. You can continue accepting the financial limitations you've inherited, or you can start writing a different story.

You can keep managing scarcity, or you can start creating abundance.

You can remain a spectator to other people's success, or you can become the protagonist of your own financial transformation.

This isn't about getting rich quick or finding secret loopholes. It's about the patient, systematic work of changing how you think about money, then aligning your actions with your expanded vision of what's possible.

The choice is yours. The tools are in this book. The only question remaining is the one that started it all:

Why not you?

If you're ready to find out, turn the page. Your financial transformation begins now.

PART I

Mindset—"Why Not Me?"

CHAPTER 1

One Mile or a Million —The False Barrier of Distance

"The mile between Jersey City and Wall Street isn't distance—it's the belief you can cross it."

The first time I saw the towers of lower Manhattan, I was ten years old, standing barefoot on the fire escape of our four-story brick apartment building in Jersey City. My small hands gripped the rusted railings until my knuckles turned white, and I stared east into the night like I was looking at another planet.

Wall Street glowed like a fortress of gold across the Hudson River. Each illuminated window was a promise of power I couldn't even pronounce. The financial district was exactly one mile from where I stood. One mile. But from my perch in my railroad apartment, it may as well have been a million.

Over there, people in sharp suits made decisions that moved mountains of money. Over here, my mother sat at our chipped Formica table, counting crumpled dollar bills like a card dealer calculating her last hand.

Over there, kids my age probably had college funds and trust accounts. Over here, we celebrated when the lights stayed on for a full month without a shut-off notice.

I didn't resent them. But I believed deeply that their world had invisible walls designed to keep people like us on the outside looking in.

That night on the fire escape, staring at those unreachable towers, I made a decision that would define my entire life. I decided that distance—real or imagined—was just another problem to solve.

THE ANATOMY OF IMPOSSIBLE

Growing up in Jersey City in the 1980s meant learning to create something from nothing—a skill that later became my greatest asset in building wealth.

Our four-story brick building wasn't just an address; it was our entire universe. Each floor housed aunts, uncles, and cousins in a symphony of salsa music, sofrito aromas, and the thunder of a dozen kids racing up and down the stairs like we owned the place.

We were the first Hispanic family to attend St. Paul of the Cross, the local Catholic school. As we walked into that building every morning in our carefully pressed uniforms, we knew we were different. No one said anything outright, but you could feel it in the curious glances, the subtle questions about our last name, and the way parents sized up my father especially when he attended to school events.

My father—Hector Ruiz Sr.—carried himself like he belonged everywhere he went. He was/is six-foot-two with raw charisma and was always wrapped in a crisp guayabera shirt. He commanded attention without demanding it. When he walked into a room, the gravity shifted. People listened not because they had to, but because they wanted to hear what came next.

At twenty, he moved from Puerto Rico with nothing but an Army discharge and an unshakeable belief that "impossible" only meant "not yet attempted." The businesses he started—restaurants, tire shops, security companies—failed spectacularly. But he kept going, and each failure taught him something new about what success meant.

"Success isn't about avoiding failure," he told me, as his calloused hands gestured over a stack of unpaid invoices. "It's about failing forward faster than the other guy gives up."

His philosophy would later become one of my core investment principles: the market rewards those who can maintain long-term perspective instead of those who panic over short-term volatility.

THE STREETS THAT BUILT MILLIONAIRES

Our playground was the block. We played stickball in the alley, manhunt in the shadows between parked cars, and handball off the brick walls at P.S. 28. We rode our bikes like they were Ferraris and weaved through traffic cones and double-parked Buicks that belonged to neighbors, who worked double shifts to make ends meet.

Summer smelled like tar and sweat and the distant promise of Mister Softee's musical ice cream truck that announced salvation in the form of frozen sugar. Winter meant snowball fights and cardboard sleds on iced-over stairs that would probably get us sued today.

We didn't have much, but we had something money couldn't buy; resourcefulness that could make Silicon Valley entrepreneurs weep with envy.

When the bat broke during our summer games, we wrapped it with electrical tape and kept playing. When the ball got lost in traffic, we made a new one from aluminum foil and rubber bands. When the rich kids wouldn't let us use their basketball court at the park, we nailed a milk crate to a telephone pole and created our own Madison Square Garden.

Looking back, I realize the streets taught us millionaire skills that were disguised as survival:

Opportunity recognition: One time we turned an abandoned lot into a baseball field by clearing debris and marking bases with stolen traffic cones. We spotted solutions where others saw problems. That's entrepreneurship 101.

Resource optimization: We learned to make Halloween costumes from garbage bags and cardboard and created elaborate characters that rivaled store-bought costumes that cost ten times more. We maximized output with minimal input. That's efficiency at its purest.

Creative problem-solving: When we couldn't afford video games, we invented elaborate fantasy games using dice and our imagination to create entertainment that lasted for hours. We found unconventional paths to conventional goals. That's innovation born from necessity.

Emotional resilience: When we scraped our knees, we quickly got back up again. Failure wasn't devastating; it was just data for the next attempt. Every scraped knee was a lesson in risk management. We learned how to bounce back from setbacks without losing momentum.

Network effects: We understood that success is a team sport. Everyone looked out for everyone else's kids. Information flowed freely and resources were shared. We learned that success is celebrated collectively.

The tragedy is that most people who develop these skills in childhood abandon them in adulthood. They start believing that "professional" success requires formal processes and expensive resources. They trade their greatest strength—scrappy creativity—for the illusion of legitimacy.

But wealth isn't built by following someone else's playbook. It's built by writing your own.

THE INVISIBLE WEIGHT OF SCARCITY

That feeling of limitation wasn't just in my imagination—it was real, palpable, and shaped every interaction in our household like humidity shapes weather.

It showed up in how my mother's shoulders tensed when the mail arrived. How conversations about money happened in hushed tones after we kids went to bed. The word "expensive" could end any conversation about wants versus needs faster than a referee's whistle.

I didn't know what "scarcity mindset" meant back then, but I felt it like a physical presence. It was heavy, inescapable, and affected everything including our grocery choices and our dreams.

It lived in the space between what we had and what we needed. It whispered in my ear every time I asked for something and watched my mother pause, while she calculated whether we could afford it. It made every financial decision feel like a zero-sum game, where choosing one thing meant losing another.

You know what I'm talking about. Maybe you've felt it too.

That knot in your stomach when bills arrive. That flush of shame when your card gets declined at the grocery store. That moment of panic when an unexpected expense shatters your fragile financial balance like when a rock cracks glass.

These aren't just feelings—they're teachers. They're shaping how you think about money right now, today, even if your bank account tells a different story than it did when you were younger.

Because here's what nobody tells you: **Scarcity isn't a temporary condition. It becomes a permanent lens through which you see the world.**

And until you change that lens, you can make all the money in the world and still feel poor.

I've seen millionaires who hoard canned food because they can't shake the childhood fear of hunger. I've worked with executives earning high six figures who panic when their balance dips below $20,000. I've coached business owners who never enjoy their success because they're always waiting for everything to collapse like a house of cards.

That's not about numbers. That's about narrative.

It's about the story you tell yourself about money—and what you believe is possible for someone like you.

THE CONVERSATION THAT CRACKED EVERYTHING OPEN

The trajectory of my life changed in a Prudential office building during what was supposed to be a gap year before law school.

I was working on a class action lawsuit that involved sales misconduct—I still technically worked "in the law" but was instead surrounded by financial analysts instead of attorneys. The energy was different in that room. It was electric in a way that made the courthouse feel like a morgue. I learned that lawyers looked backwards at problems that had already happened, while financial analysts looked forward at possibilities yet to be created.

The building itself pulsed with a different kind of urgency. People moved with purpose rather than bureaucratic routine. Conversations buzzed with terms I didn't understand; like basis points, alpha generation, correlation coefficients. It was like being in a foreign country where everyone spoke fluent opportunity.

One afternoon, a senior advisor named Richard noticed me reading mutual fund literature at my desk during lunch break. I was probably the only 22-year-old in America voluntarily studying expense ratios.

"You thinking about investing?" he asked, settling into the chair next to my cubicle with the casual confidence of someone who'd made this conversation profitable many times before.

I laughed the same nervous laugh I had perfected when people assumed I belonged in spaces I never imagined entering. "I'm pre-law. And besides... I don't have that kind of money."

He tilted his head with the patience of someone who'd heard this response a thousand times before. "How much do you think it takes to start investing?"

"I don't know... tens of thousands? Enough to make it worthwhile."

Richard smiled and opened a spreadsheet on his computer. "If you invest two hundred dollars a month starting now, you'll have over a million dollars by the time you're sixty."

I smirked as I became certain he was setting up some kind of sales pitch. He didn't.

Instead, he showed me the mathematics of compound growth. These numbers soon haunted my dreams and reshaped my destiny. Line by line, year by year, the numbers climbed like a staircase to the impossible. At 8% annual returns, my $200 monthly contributions would total $240,000 over thirty years, but the account would be worth over $1 million.

"The first year, you contribute $2,400 and end up with maybe $2,600," he explained, his finger tracing the early years where progress felt painfully slow. "Doesn't feel like much. But by year fifteen, you're contributing the same $2,400, but your account grows by $15,000 that year. By year thirty, your annual growth is larger than most people's salaries."

Then he leaned back and said something that shattered every assumption I carried about money throughout my childhood:

"The biggest difference between wealthy people and broke people isn't discipline or income or luck. It's how they frame opportunity. You were taught to see risk. I was taught to see potential."

In that moment, the frame cracked.

The story I'd carried since childhood—that wealth was for "them" and working-class survival was for "us"—suddenly felt optional instead of inevitable.

THE GAP YEAR THAT OPENED EVERYTHING

What was supposed to be a simple year between undergrad and law school became an awakening I never saw coming.

Every day in that Prudential building exposed me to a different way of thinking about money that felt like learning a new language. I watched traders make split-second decisions involving millions of dollars with the same casual precision my father used to negotiate tire prices. I sat in on meetings where portfolio managers discussed risk and return like engineers discussing bridge specifications—technical, precise, unemotional.

I started volunteering for projects that put me in rooms with the investment team, soaking up conversations like a sponge absorbing water. I began reading financial publications during lunch breaks, trying to decode terms like "efficient frontier" and "alpha generation" like they were ancient hieroglyphics. I asked annoying questions about how markets worked, how portfolios were constructed, and how ordinary people became wealthy.

The more I learned, the more I realized how much I didn't know—not just about finance, but about the psychology of money itself.

I discovered that most people make financial decisions emotionally and then rationalize them logically, like buying a sports car and then explaining why it's "practical transportation", or that most investment returns come from asset allocation rather than security selection—boring things that works better than exciting stuff that crashes. That time in the market beats timing the market with remarkable consistency, despite what financial television would have you believe.

But the biggest revelation was this: **Wealth building is a system, not a secret.**

It's not about finding the perfect stock, or timing the market, or having access to exclusive opportunities reserved for the rich and famous. It's about understanding a few fundamental principles and then having the discipline to apply them consistently over time.

That realization was both liberating and terrifying. Liberating because it meant wealth was accessible to anyone willing to learn and apply the system. Terrifying because it meant I had no excuse not to try.

THE HARDEST CONVERSATION I'VE EVER HAD

Telling my father that I wasn't going to law school felt like betraying a sacred covenant written in sacrifice and dreams.

Law school represented everything he had sacrificed for—stability, prestige, and the promise that his son would never have to build businesses with his hands like he had. My brothers had already walked that path successfully and became an attorney who could afford nice cars and homes in safe neighborhoods. I was meant to be the third attorney in the family, the final piece of his American dream.

We sat across from each other at the same kitchen table where I'd asked my mother about making more money instead of stretching less. The same table where she'd counted bills and calculated miracles with the precision of a NASA engineer. My hands were shaking as I spoke, and I could feel the weight of generations of expectations pressing down on my shoulders.

"I'm not going to law school, Dad. I'm going into finance."

The silence stretched between us like a chasm. His face cycled through confusion, disappointment, and something that looked like grief for the path not taken. I watched him process the words and see the collapse of a carefully constructed plan he had been building for twenty-two years.

"Why?" he finally asked, his voice steady but strained, like a man trying not to show how much the blow had hurt.

I took a deep breath and tried to explain something to him that I was still figuring out myself. "Because I've found something that matters more. A way to help families like ours build wealth, not just income. Something that feels like what I was made to do."

"But law is secure," he said, his hands gesturing toward some invisible future of certainty. "It's respected. It's what we planned."

"I know, Dad. And I understand why that matters to you. But I think I can do more good this way. I think I can help people who grew up like we did but never had anyone to teach them how money really works."

Another long pause. The kitchen clock ticked like a metronome counting the seconds until my life changed forever.

"Are you sure about this?"

"No," I admitted, my voice barely above a whisper. "I'm scared. But I'm more scared of not trying."

Then he said something that gave me permission to become myself:

"I didn't come to this country for my children to become just like me. I came so they could become themselves."

In that moment, I learned that the greatest gift a parent can give isn't a predetermined path—it's the courage to forge your own.

But the conversation wasn't over. He leaned forward, his voice taking on the tone he used when teaching me important life lessons.

"If you're going to do this, you need to understand something about money that I learned the hard way. Money isn't just numbers on a page. It's power. It's freedom. It's dignity.

But it's also responsibility. If you're going to help other people with their money, you better understand your own first."

That advice would prove prophetic in ways I had not yet imagined.

FROM GUT FEELINGS TO GUIDED GROWTH

That conversation didn't just change my career—it launched my mission to bridge the gap between financial knowledge and financial freedom.

I threw myself into studying everything about finance and behavioral economics like a possessed man. I got licensed (Series 6, 63, and eventually Series 7), but more importantly, I started studying the psychology of money—the hidden forces that drive people to make decisions that sabotage their own success.

I discovered that most financial advice fails because it treats people like calculators instead of humans. Traditional approaches focus on mathematical optimization, while ignoring the psychological and emotional forces that drive behavior.

For example, the standard advice to "buy low, sell high" is mathematically correct, but psychologically impossible for most people. When markets are crashing (prices are low), human emotions scream "sell before you lose everything." When markets are soaring (prices are high), greed whispers, "Buy before you miss out."

This is the key insight that shaped my entire approach: **Successful investing isn't about controlling markets—it's about controlling yourself.**

This led me to study behavioral finance pioneers, like Daniel Kahneman and Richard Thaler, to learn about cognitive biases that hijack rational decision-making:

Loss aversion: The tendency to prefer avoiding losses over acquiring equivalent gains. This concept explains why people keep too much money in low-yielding savings accounts. The fear of potential investment losses can overwhelm the rational understanding of inflation's guaranteed erosion of purchasing power.

Confirmation bias: The tendency to search for and interpret information that confirms existing beliefs. This is why some people only read financial news that supports their predetermined views about the market.

Recency bias: The choice to overweigh recent events when making decisions. This drives people to pile into investments that have recently performed well, often buying at peak prices.

Understanding these patterns was not just academic—it became the foundation of how I help clients build wealth. Instead of fighting human nature, I learned to work with it.

THE MILLIONAIRE MAILMAN AND THE PHYSICS OF WEALTH

Years later, I learned that one of the postal workers in my neighborhood had quietly built his portfolio.

James delivered mail for thirty years and never earned more than $65,000 annually. But every paycheck, he bought shares of dividend-growing companies and reinvested every cent. He never sold during crashes, never chased hot tips, and never tried to time the market.

When he invited me to his retirement party, I couldn't hide my curiosity about his investment approach.

"The stock market is the only store where when everything goes on sale, everyone runs out screaming," he told me with a chuckle, his eyes twinkling with the wisdom of someone who had cracked the code.

His strategy was beautifully simple:

- **Systematic investing**: $500 every month, regardless of market conditions, economic headlines, or his own emotions
- **Dividend focus**: Companies with long histories of increasing payouts, the aristocrats of American business
- **Automatic reinvestment**: Every dividend bought more shares, creating a compounding snowball effect
- **Infinite patience**: Never sold a single share in thirty years, riding out every crash and correction
- **Emotional discipline**: Ignored market noise and media hysteria like they were background static

By retirement, his dividend income exceeded both his pension and Social Security combined. He had discovered what I now call the physics of wealth: **consistent action plus compound time equals extraordinary results.**

James proved what I'd suspected since that conversation with Richard: wealth isn't about how much you make—it's about how you think about what you make.

His story became a case study I share with every client who thinks wealth building requires high income or sophisticated strategies. Sometimes the most powerful approach is also the simplest.

THE MOMENT EVERYTHING CRYSTALLIZED

The full impact of my career choice didn't hit me until I was sitting across from my first real client, a young teacher named Maria, who reminded me of my mother in ways that made my chest tight.

She was twenty-six, single, and earning $38,000 per year teaching middle school kids who probably made more in allowance than she made in a week. She'd saved $5,000 and wanted to know if she could start investing. Her biggest fear wasn't market volatility—it was making a mistake that would wipe out everything she'd worked to save.

"I don't know anything about this stuff," she said, her voice carrying the same uncertainty I'd felt in that Prudential office years earlier. "I'm probably not the kind of person who invests."

I leaned forward and said something that surprised us both: "You're exactly the kind of person who should invest. You're young, you're disciplined enough to save money on a teacher's salary, and you understand the value of every dollar. Those are the only qualifications that matter."

We started with a simple plan: $200 per month into a diversified index fund. Nothing fancy. Nothing complex. Just consistent, systematic investing designed to grow with the market over time.

Five years later, she called to tell me her portfolio had grown to over $18,000, which was more money than she'd ever imagined having in one account. But more importantly, she'd stopped thinking of herself as someone who "couldn't understand money." She'd become an investor.

Her transformation from fear to confidence, from scarcity to abundance thinking reminded me why I had chosen this path. I wasn't just managing money; I was changing lives by changing how people thought about their financial potential.

THE DISTANCE THAT REALLY MATTERS

Looking back now, I know the distance between where I started and where I am today was never measured in miles.

It was measured in mindsets.

The physical distance from Jersey City to Wall Street is trivial. Technically, it is a quick PATH train ride that costs $2.75 and takes twelve minutes. But the psychological distance felt infinite until I learned to see it differently.

For some people, success is a straight highway where the path is paved, the destination is clear, and all they have to do is drive. But for those of us who start far from traditional opportunities, the journey feels like climbing an unmarked mountain in a fog, with no map and no guarantee that there is anything waiting for us at the top.

Here's what I've learned after helping hundreds of families build wealth: **the biggest limitation isn't where you start—it's what you believe is possible from where you're standing.**

Every opportunity that feels "out of reach" is actually just waiting for you to reach differently—with better questions, clearer thinking, and the courage to challenge the stories that have been limiting your vision.

At every stage of my career, I closed the gap between my current reality and my growing goals by refusing to accept that distance was permanent. Each time I felt intimidated by a new environment or challenge, I reminded myself that everyone in that room had started somewhere too. The partner at Ernst & Young who intimidated me during my interview had once been a nervous college graduate wondering if he was smart enough. The portfolio manager who seemed to effortlessly discuss complex strategies had once struggled to understand basic concepts. The successful entrepreneurs I now advise had once been employees afraid to take risks.

Distance is often just unfamiliarity in disguise.

THE POWER OF PROXY EXPERIENCES

One of the most powerful tools for closing psychological distance is what I call "proxy experiences", which is finding examples of people who started where you are and ended up where you want to be.

When I was struggling to believe I belonged in high-level financial discussions, I studied the backgrounds of successful advisors and money managers. I was surprised to discover how many came from modest backgrounds, immigrant families, or other non-traditional paths that looked nothing like the privileged narratives I'd imagined.

Warren Buffett grew up in Omaha, not Manhattan, and started his investment company from his bedroom. John Bogle founded Vanguard after being fired from his previous job. Suze Orman was a waitress until age thirty before becoming a financial advisor.

These weren't superhuman geniuses with special advantages or trust funds. They were people who learned to think differently about money and then had the persistence to act on that new thinking when others gave up.

I started collecting both famous and personal stories, like the postal worker who built wealth through dividend investing or the teacher who became a millionaire through systematic saving, and the small business owner who created generational wealth through strategic planning.

Each story served as proof that the distance between where you are and where you want to be isn't as far as it appears. It's just measured in different units than you think.

YOUR WALL STREET IS WAITING

That ten-year-old boy standing on the fire escape, staring at Wall Street's glowing towers, didn't know he was looking at his future office buildings. He just knew that whatever was happening over there, he wanted to understand it.

The distance between that moment and today was not conquered through luck or special advantages. It was closed through the daily choice to believe that growth was possible, learning was available, and barriers were meant to be broken.

Your Wall Street might not be a financial district. It might be:

- The business you want to start but think you're not "entrepreneurial enough" for
- The investment portfolio you want to build but think requires more money than you have
- The home you want to own but think is "out of your price range"
- The retirement you want to design but think requires more time than you have left
- The financial security you want to create but think requires knowledge you don't possess
- The legacy you want to leave but think requires wealth you'll never accumulate

Whatever it is—that thing that feels simultaneously close enough to see but too far to reach—I want you to know something crucial:

The distance is negotiable.

The only real barrier between you and your financial goals isn't external circumstances, market conditions, or economic factors, it's the story you have accepted about what is possible for someone from your background, your education, your current circumstances.

But here's the beautiful truth: Stories can be rewritten. Mindsets can be shifted. Distances can be closed.

And the most beautiful part? Once you cross that bridge yourself, you can help others cross it too.

THE COMPOUND EFFECT OF CHANGED PERSPECTIVE

When you change how you see your financial possibilities, the effects compound in ways you may not expect:

Opportunity Recognition: You start noticing investment opportunities, side income possibilities, and wealth-building strategies that were always there but invisible to your old self.

Network Expansion: You begin gravitating towards people who share your growth mindset and begin naturally building relationships with people who open doors and create possibilities.

Risk Recalibration: You start distinguishing between intelligent risks that build wealth and foolish risks that destroy it, becoming more strategic rather than more cautious.

Decision Quality: Your financial choices become more intentional and less reactive, leading to better outcomes over time.

Emotional Regulation: Market volatility and temporary setbacks become data points rather than crisis moments, allowing you to maintain long-term perspective.

These shifts don't happen overnight, but they're inevitable once you commit to seeing money differently. It's like learning a new language—awkward at first but eventually becoming second nature.

FROM "SOMEDAY" TO "DAY ONE"

The greatest tragedy in personal finance isn't market crashes or bad investments—it's the paralysis that keeps people from starting.

I see it every day: people waiting for the "perfect" moment, the bigger salary, the clearer path. They treat wealth building like a luxury that they cannot afford, instead of the necessity it is.

But here's the truth that changed everything for me: **There is no perfect moment. There is only this moment and what you choose to do with it.**

That ten-year-old boy on the fire escape didn't wait for permission to dream bigger. He did not let distance define his limits. He asked a simple question that changed everything:

"Why not me?"

Now it's your turn to ask the same question. Not someday. Not when you're ready. Not when the conditions are perfect.

Today.

Because the only thing standing between you and the financial life you want is the story you've been telling yourself about what's possible.

And stories? Stories can be rewritten.

Starting now.

CHAPTER 2

The Cash Flow Command Center

"Your cash flow isn't just numbers
—it's the engine that powers your dreams."

WHERE YOUR MONEY LEARNS TO DANCE INSTEAD OF STUMBLE

The night I discovered that cash flow wasn't a spreadsheet, but a story, I was sitting at a chipped kitchen table, listening to the sound of a cheap box fan push heavy summer air around my cramped apartment. A rent notice teetered on the edge, and a grocery receipt lay under my elbow. Besides my hands, there was a calculator that had seen better decades.

I didn't feel broke. I felt **blurry**. Blurry is dangerous when it comes to money. You can't steer what you can't see clearly.

So, I drew it out like a mapmaker charting unknown territory. **Income** wasn't just numbers deposited into checking accounts; it was *streams* flowing toward me—streams that could be widened, redirected, or multiplied. **Expenses** weren't bills demanding payment; they were *choices*, habits dressed up in monthly invoices that had convinced me they were necessities. **Savings** were not what was left over after everything else—it was a *line item with a mission*. And debt? Debt was tomorrow's money rented at today's anxiety rate.

That night, everything changed. I stopped managing money and started orchestrating it.

THE CASH-FLOW MIRROR

Your budget isn't a punishment device designed to make you feel guilty about buying coffee. It's a mirror. The question isn't "Where did all my money go?" The question is **"What story am I funding with my spending?"**

When I ask clients to do a first-pass audit, I give them four highlighters and a simple instruction: color-code your last three months of expenses.

- **Green** for *Grow* (investments, education, skill building—anything that makes future-you wealthier or wiser)
- **Blue** for *Bills* (fixed essentials that keep life stable —rent, utilities, insurance, groceries)
- **Yellow** for *Joy* (the things that make life worth living —travel, hobbies, experiences, the good wine)
- **Red** for *Drag* (interest payments, fees, unused subscriptions, habitual leaks that serve no purpose except making other people rich)

Most people are stunned by what they discover. Their spending is not immoral — it is **aimless**. They are often not bad with money; they just never told their money where to go, so it wandered off.

The fix isn't austerity. It's **aim**. We don't cut joy. We cut, drag, and reassign those dollars for growth.

THE 50/30/20 (AND HOW TO EVOLVE BEYOND IT)

Rules of thumb work beautifully, until you outgrow them. The classic **50/30/20** framework of "Needs / Wants / Saving & Debt" is a solid starting point for someone moving from reactive to intentional money management. But as your capacity grows, I like to evolve clients to **50/20/20/10**:

- **50% Needs** (the non-negotiable core that keeps your life functioning)
- **20% Investing and Saving** (automated wealth building that you never see or miss)
- **20% Freedom Fund** (joy, travel, memory-making, the stuff that makes you glad to be alive)
- **10% Futureproofing** (insurance, property maintenance reserves, career upskilling—the buffer between you and life's surprises)

That last bucket is what separates people who weather storms, from people who get destroyed by them. It is the space between you and panic.

Practice Drill: Reallocate the Raise The next time you receive a raise, split it immediately by 50% to lifestyle improvement, 50% to investing / saving. If you cannot feel the raise improving your daily life, you will not sustain the new savings rate. If you don't invest half, inflation will eat it anyway.

THE TWO-ACCOUNT RULE (SAFETY & STRATEGY)

Here's a fundamental principle that will transform your relationship with money: **Separate Safety from Strategy**.

Safety is your fortress. Be sure to have 3 to 12 months of essential expenses, calibrated to your job stability and number of dependents, saved. Strategy is your investment engine—money specifically deployed to grow wealth over time.

- **Safety account rule:** It doesn't apologize for «low yield.» Its job isn't to make you rich; its job is to let you sleep at night.
- **Strategy account rule:** Money moves here on a predetermined schedule, not based on your feelings about the market.

Name these accounts in your banking app like the following: "Family Fortress" for Safety and "Wealth Builder" for Strategy. Your brain protects what it names with intention.

INCOME IS A DESIGN VARIABLE

We spend endless energy optimizing expenses and almost none designing bigger income streams. My income jumped dramatically when I stopped asking, *"How can I make more money?"* and started asking, **"How can I become more useful to more people?"**

Usefulness scales. The market pays premium prices for solutions to painful problems, not for hours on a time clock.

The 14-Day Solution Memo: List three problems you can solve at a high level—problems that keep people awake at night or cost them significant money. For each problem, write a 200-word memo titled «How I Would Solve This in 14 Days.» Send one memo per week to someone who has that exact problem. You are one well-aimed memo away from a different income bracket.

Case Study: "Keys for Keisha" Keisha managed properties for small landlords but felt trapped in an hourly wage cage. Instead of looking for a new job, we redesigned her usefulness. She packaged her tenant-turnover playbook into a systemized service and started selling it to other small landlords for a fixed fee plus consultation retainer. Income increased 43% in nine months. Same person, exponentially larger usefulness footprint.

DEBT: LEVERS VS. LABELS

Not all debt carries the same DNA. Debt used to acquire appreciating assets or durable earning power (i.e. thoughtfully chosen education, a business with real unit economics, income-producing real estate) functions as a **lever**, meaning it amplifies your wealth-building capacity. Revolving consumer debt functions as a **label**—a nametag that says, *"I'm buying speed with tomorrow's regret."*

HIERARCHY OF PAYOFF PRIORITY:

1. **Toxic Debt** (high-interest credit cards, payday loans) attack with religious intensity

2. **Expensive Debt** (auto loans >6-7%, personal loans) accelerate payoff once toxic debt is eliminated
3. **Neutral Debt** (mortgages at reasonable rates, some student loans) service as agreed while maximizing investment contributions

Choose to **snowball method:** Pay off the smallest balance first., if you need psychological wins to maintain momentum. Choose to **avalanche method**: Pay off highest interest rate first) if mathematical optimization motivates you. The correct method is the one you will surely complete.

Micro-Tactic: Call your credit card company after three consecutive on-time payments and request a rate review. Script: *"I'm consolidating my debt and want to maintain our relationship. Can you review my APR and waive any fees to help me pay this off faster?"* Success rate is surprisingly high.

Case Study: "Miguel vs. the Minimums" Miguel carried four credit cards and a personal loan, making minimum payments that barely dented principal balances. We organized debts by interest rate, automated the avalanche approach, and funded the offensive by selling two idle toys from his garage for $1,700. Twelve months later: zero revolving debt and a credit score improvement that qualified him for a car refinance, dropping his monthly payment by $92, allowing money to flow directly into his investments.

EMERGENCY FUNDS THAT ACTUALLY FUNCTION

"Save three to six months of expenses" is financial advice for people who like their guidance vague. It is crucial to build your safety net based on **job volatility, number of**

dependents, single vs. dual income, and **fixed obligations**. Contractors, commission-based earners, and single-income households often need 9-12 months of coverage. People with tenure-track positions may need less.

SAFETY NET ARCHITECTURE

- Keep one month of expenses in checking account as operational buffer
- Keep the remainder in high-yield savings or short-term Treasury bill ladder
- Rebuild the fortress first after any emergency—don't "catch up on investing" by letting safety wither

Naming Power: Rename your emergency fund. «Family Fortress» creates stronger psychological protection than «Savings Account #4.» You'll guard it more fiercely because it protects people you love.

THE WEALTH OPERATING RHYTHM

Money loves rhythm and withers under chaos. Without consistent review cycles, life will spend your next raise before you even know you got it.

- **Weekly (15 minutes):** Scan account balances, upcoming bills, any fraud alerts
- **Monthly (45 minutes):** Reconcile expenses, redirect recovered waste to growth accounts, review automated transfers

- **Quarterly (90 minutes):** Portfolio checkup against target allocation, rebalance, if necessary, execute tax-loss harvesting
- **Yearly (half-day retreat):** Big picture visioning—goals review, insurance updates, estate document refresh, career trajectory assessment, education funding, charitable planning

Friction Elimination: Put every fixed bill on autopay from a dedicated checking account. Fund this account immediately on payday. One account for living expenses, one for bills, one for financial experiments. Your calendar becomes your CFO.

THE DRAG HUNT (30-MINUTE WEALTH RECOVERY)

Open your last two bank statements and circle these wealth leaks:

- Subscriptions you have not used in 60 days (unused gym memberships, streaming services, software licenses)
- Fees of any kind (bank fees, ATM charges, late payment penalties)—call and request reversal
- Insurance premiums—request competitive quotes every 24 months; loyalty rarely pays
- Phone / internet bills—call the retention department annually for "longtime customer" discounts

Total the recovered amount and assign it immediately to your Wealth Builder account. Celebrate by renaming that budget line **"Reclaimed Money to Freedom."**

THREE TRANSFORMATION STORIES, PROOF BEATS PLATITUDES

Maria, the Teacher (Age 26): Saved $5,000 but was convinced she «wasn't the investing type.» We automated $200/month into a diversified index fund. Five years later: $18,000+ portfolio, but more importantly, a completely new identity—*wealth builder*. Story changed → Actions changed → Results changed.

Andrés, the Contractor (Age 41): Cash flow was feast-or-famine seasonality. We built a *Jobs Pipeline Calendar* and a **Future-Proofing** fund for equipment repairs and slow seasons. Anxiety decreased, confidence increased, bids rose. He could now price with certainty instead of desperation, and his income steadied.

Saira, RN (Age 33): Wanted to buy a home *and* return to graduate school, which appeared to mutually exclusive goals on a nurse's salary. We mapped her cash flow to seasonal phases: 12 months of debt elimination and fortress building, followed by aggressive investment ramping, and followed by strategic preparation for school. She achieved both goals without financial stress fractures.

SCRIPTS FOR IMMEDIATE IMPLEMENTATION

- **Pay Yourself First Mentality:** *"I move 15% to wealth building on the 1st of every month, because my future deserves the first cut, not the leftovers."*
- **Bill Negotiation Script:** *"Is there a loyalty discount or promotional rate you can extend to maintain our relationship?"*

- **Income Expansion Ask:** *"I noticed [specific problem] in your process. If I could eliminate that issue in 14 days, would that be worth $[X] to your business?"*

YOUR 10-DAY CASH-FLOW TRANSFORMATION SPRINT

Day 1: Rename your accounts: «Family Fortress» (safety) and «Wealth Builder» (strategy)

Day 2: Set up automatic transfers to occur monthly on a specific date

Day 3: Execute the **Drag Hunt**—cancel, negotiate, or transfer every wasteful expense

Day 4: Choose your **50/20/20/10** targets based on current income

Day 5: Write and send your first 14-Day Solution Memo to a potential client

Day 6: List all debts by interest rate, choose snowball or avalanche, and automate the attack

Day 7: Create a dedicated bills-only checking account and transfer all fixed payments there

Day 8: Build a 12-month view of irregular expenses (insurance premiums, travel, car maintenance) and create monthly set-asides to smooth cash flow

Day 9: Schedule your Weekly / Monthly / Quarterly / Yearly review appointments in your calendar

Day 10: Celebrate a small victory using money from your **Freedom Fund.** Anchor this new system in joy, not deprivation.

THE DANCE BEGINS NOW

Money is less about mathematical precision than financial choreography. Once you establish the steps, the dance becomes natural, and even graceful. Your budget isn't a cage designed to limit you; it's a compass pointing toward a life you recognize as authentically yours.

Remember that blurry feeling that brought me to the kitchen table with a calculator and a rent notice? It transformed into clarity, then confidence, then the ability to help others find their own rhythm.

Your money is waiting to learn the steps. The music has already started.

Time to dance.

CHAPTER 3

The Psychology of Wealth —Rewiring Your Money Mind

"Scarcity rewires your mind—break the lens, and wealth becomes your new vision."

YOUR MIND IS THE LOCK. WEALTH WAITS ON THE OTHER SIDE.

At 2:47 AM on a Tuesday, my phone buzzed with a text that would change how I understand money forever:

"Can't sleep. Been thinking about our conversation. I think I know why I keep sabotaging myself financially. It's not about the numbers. It's about what I think I deserve."

The message was from Maria, the 26-year-old teacher I had been working with for six months. Despite having a solid financial plan and the income to execute it, she kept making decisions that undermined her own progress. She'd save $500, then blow it on clothes she didn't need. She would start investing and then panic and cash out during minor market dips. She would commit to a budget and then abandon it after two weeks.

I'd seen the pattern before, but Maria's late-night revelation crystallized something crucial: **The biggest barriers to building wealth aren't mathematical—they are psychological.**

Your net worth is not just a reflection of your financial decisions. It is a mirror of your internal beliefs about money, success, and what you think you deserve in life.

THE ENEMY LIVES INSIDE THE HOUSE

Growing up, Maria had absorbed a series of unconscious beliefs about money that were now running her financial life like malicious software:

- *Belief #1:"Good people don't care about money"* (so wanting wealth made her feel guilty)
- *Belief #2: "Rich people are greedy"* (so accumulating wealth felt like becoming someone she didn't want to be)
- *Belief #3: "Money causes problems"* (so her subconscious protected her from wealth to avoid conflict)
- *Belief #4: "I'm not the type of person who has money"* (so any financial success felt temporary and fake)

These were not conscious thoughts. They were buried programs running in the background that sabotaged every good intention and smart strategy.

The moment I realized this, everything about financial planning changed for me. I stopped focusing exclusively on the mechanics of money and started paying attention to the psychology of wealth.

THE THREE PSYCHOLOGICAL GATEKEEPERS

After working with hundreds of clients, I've identified three primary psychological barriers that keep people trapped in financial mediocrity:

Gatekeeper #1, The Scarcity Guardian: *"There's never enough. Taking more means someone else gets less."*

Gatekeeper #2, The Unworthiness Warden: *"People like me don't deserve financial success. We should be grateful for what we have."*

Gatekeeper #3, The Fear Fortress: *"If I try and fail, I'll prove I'm not capable. Better to not try at all."*

Each gatekeeper has a specific job: protecting you from the imagined dangers of pursuing wealth. However, it is important to remember they are using outdated security protocols based on childhood experiences that no longer serve you.

SCARCITY: THE LIE THAT POVERTY IS VIRTUOUS

Scarcity thinking isn't about having limited resources, it is about believing that limitation is permanent and personal. It is the voice that whispers *"Who are you to want more?"* every time you consider upgrading your financial life.

I learned this from watching my own mother, who could perform miracles with $37 until payday but also could not imagine a world where money wasn't a constant source of stress. She had trained herself to be brilliant at managing shortage, but terrible at creating abundance.

The Scarcity Test: Notice your internal reaction to these statements,

- "I want to earn $100,000 this year"
- "I deserve to have financial freedom"
- "I'm going to build wealth and enjoy it"

If any part of yourself cringes, argues, or feels uncomfortable, it is now clear that scarcity thinking is running your financial show.

SCARCITY REHABILITATION PROTOCOL:

Step 1: Identify the Source Story

When did you first learn that wanting money was wrong? What story were you told about people who have wealth? Write it down. Name it. Examine it as an external idea, not as an internal truth.

Step 2: Rewrite the Narrative

Replace scarcity scripts with abundance truths,

- Old: "Money is the root of all evil" → New: "Money is a tool that amplifies who you already are"
- Old: "Rich people are greedy" → New: "Wealthy people have more capacity to create value and solve problems"
- Old: "I should be content with what I have" → New: "I can be grateful for what I have while building toward what I want"

Step 3: Practice Abundance Thinking Daily

Every morning, list three financial opportunities available to you today. Train your brain to notice possibilities instead of limitations.

UNWORTHINESS: THE IMPOSTOR IN YOUR INVESTMENT ACCOUNT

Unworthiness is the voice that says *"This success isn't real. They're going to figure out I don't belong here."* It is the reason people unconsciously sabotage their financial progress just when things start working.

I see this constantly. The entrepreneur who finally starts making money, then immediately finds ways to spend it all. The investor who builds a portfolio, then panics, and sells just before it takes off. The professional who gets promoted, then engages in self-destructive behavior that torpedoes the opportunity.

Unworthiness doesn't want you to fail—it wants to protect you from the imagined consequences of success. This "protection" is killing your potential.

THE WORTHINESS RECALIBRATION PROCESS

Evidence Collection: Create a «Success Inventory». Begin documenting every financial win you've ever had, no matter how small. You can start with writing down the time you saved money for something you wanted, or the bill you successfully paid off, or the raise you negotiated. Your brain needs evidence that you're capable of financial success.

Future Self Visualization: Spend 10 minutes daily visualizing yourself as someone who naturally and easily manages wealth. See yourself making investment decisions with confidence. Feel what it's like to have financial choices. Don't focus on the money and instead focus on the person you will become when money is no longer a source of stress.

Worthiness Affirmations: Replace unworthiness programming with ownership statements:

- "I create value in the world and deserve to be compensated well for it"
- "My financial success enables me to help more people"
- "I am naturally good with money and getting better every day"

FEAR: THE PARALYSIS THAT MASQUERADES AS PRUDENCE

Fear is the most sophisticated of the psychological gatekeepers because it disguises itself as wisdom. It convinces you that not taking financial risks is the safest choice, when the biggest risk is standing still while inflation and opportunity costs compound against you.

The Fear Audit: Ask yourself these questions:

- What financial opportunity am I avoiding because I'm afraid of losing money?
- What would I do with my money if I knew I couldn't fail?

- What story am I telling myself about why I can't afford to invest/start a business/ask for a raise?

FEAR TRANSFORMATION THROUGH GRADUATED EXPOSURE

Level 1: Start Stupidly Small

If investing terrifies you, start with $25. If starting a business feels impossible, spend one hour on a business idea. The goal is not obtaining results, it's proving to yourself that you can take action in spite of fear.

Level 2: Educate Away the Mystery

Fear thrives on ignorance, so read one investment book, or take one business course, or talk to one successful person in your field. Remember, knowledge is fear's natural enemy.

Level 3: Build Your "Failure Resume"

Start learning from failed investments that taught you lessons. Write down a time where you had failed financially and still survived. Business ideas that didn't work but gave you experience. Your brain needs evidence that failure isn't fatal.

THE WEALTH IDENTITY SHIFT

The most powerful psychological transformation happens when you stop seeing yourself as someone who "has money problems" and start seeing yourself as someone who "builds wealth".

This is not just positive thinking, it is identity engineering.

Old Identity: «I'm bad with money»
New Identity: «I'm learning to build wealth»

Old Identity: «I can't afford that»
New Identity: «How can I afford that?»

Old Identity: «Rich people are different from me»
New Identity: «I'm studying how wealth builders think»

THE MIRROR EXERCISE

Every morning for 30 days, look in the mirror and say: *"I am a wealth builder. I make smart financial decisions. Money flows to me because I create value for others."*

Although this feels ridiculous at first, do it anyways. Your subconscious does not distinguish between reality and repeated statements. Through this exercise, you will reprogram your financial operating system.

SOCIAL ENVIRONMENT ARCHITECTURE

You adopt the habits of the five people you spend the most time with—including their financial beliefs. If you're surrounded by people who complain about money, avoid financial planning, and believe wealth is impossible, their mindset becomes your ceiling.

WEALTH CIRCLE DESIGN

- **Subtract:** Limit time with people who drain your financial ambition
- **Add:** Seek out people who are building wealth or already have it

- **Multiply:** Join investment clubs, business groups, or online communities focused on financial growth

THE MONEY STORY REWRITE

Your current financial reality is the result of the story you've been telling yourself about money. To change your reality, you must first change your story.

Current Story Audit: Write down your current money story in one paragraph. What do you believe about money? About people who have it? About your ability to build wealth?

New Story Creation: Rewrite your money story as if you're the hero of your own financial adventure. What obstacles will you overcome? What skills will you develop? What impact will you create with your wealth?

Daily Story Reinforcement: Read your new money story every morning for 90 days. Your brain will start organizing your behavior around this new narrative.

THE COMPOUND EFFECT OF MINDSET CHANGES

When you shift from scarcity to abundance thinking, extraordinary things begin to happen:

- You notice investment opportunities you previously missed
- You ask for raises and promotions with confidence
- You start businesses instead of just thinking about them

- You make financial decisions based on potential upside instead of fear of downside
- You learn how money becomes a tool for creating the life you want instead of a source of stress

IMPLEMENTATION PROTOCOL: THE 30-DAY MIND SHIFT

Week 1: Awareness Building

- Complete the psychological gatekeeper's assessment
- Write your current money story
- Begin daily worthiness affirmations

Week 2: Pattern Interruption

- Notice and challenge scarcity thoughts as they arise
- Practice the mirror exercise daily
- Start evidence collection for your success inventory

Week 3: New Programming

- Take time daily to visualize your wealthy future
- Rewrite your money story
- Take one small financial action despite fear

Week 4: Environment Design

- Evaluate your social circle's financial influence
- Find one new person who models wealth-building behavior
- Join one community focused on financial growth

THE META-SKILL THAT CHANGES EVERYTHING

Here's what I've learned after helping hundreds of people transform their financial lives: **The ability to manage your psychology around money is more valuable than any specific financial strategy.**

Technical knowledge about investments, budgeting, and business is important, but it can be useless if your subconscious mind sabotages every good decision you try to make.

Learn to master your money psychology, and every financial tool becomes more powerful. Ignore it, and even the best strategies will fail.

YOUR NEXT ACTION STEP

Choose one psychological barrier that resonates most strongly with you right now. Commit to working on it for the next 30 days using the protocols in this chapter.

Don't try to fix everything at once. Pick one gatekeeper, focus all your energy on transforming that pattern, and watch how it changes everything else.

Your mind is the lock. But you hold the key. The only question is,

Are you ready to turn it?

PART II

MECHANICS—"BUILDING THE BLUEPRINT"

CHAPTER 4

The Four Seasons of Wealth —Your Life-Stage Investment Strategy

"Your wealth blooms in every season —plant now, or harvest nothing."

THE CALL THAT CHANGED EVERYTHING ABOUT TIMING

The phone rang at 6:23 AM on a Saturday morning. I knew before I answered that something was wrong—nobody calls that early with good news.

"Manny," said my client Robert, a construction company owner whose steady confidence had been replaced by barely contained panic. "The market just crashed twenty percent. My retirement account is bleeding money. I'm fifty-eight years old. Should I sell everything?"

This was March 2020. The world was shutting down. Markets were free-falling. And Robert—who had been methodically building wealth for two decades—was about to make the most expensive mistake of his life.

"Robert," I said, pulling on clothes while walking to my home office, "what season are you in?"

"What the hell does that mean? It's spring, but—"

"No," I interrupted. "What wealth season are you in?"

There was silence on the other end. Then, "I have no idea what you're talking about."

That conversation led to one of the most important realizations of my career: **Most people fail at wealth building not because they don't know what to do, but because they're doing the right things at the wrong time.**

Your investment strategy should change as dramatically as your wardrobe changes with the seasons. What works in the Spring of your career will destroy you in the Winter of retirement. What's conservative in Summer becomes reckless in Autumn.

Understanding your wealth season isn't just helpful—it's the difference between retiring comfortably and working until you die.

THE FOUR SEASONS FRAMEWORK: YOUR FINANCIAL GPS

Every investor moves through four distinct seasons, each with its own opportunities, challenges, and optimal strategies:

Spring (Ages 20-35): The Planting Season

- Maximum growth potential, maximum risk tolerance
- Long time horizon allows for aggressive strategies
- Focus: Accumulation and education

Summer (Ages 35-50): The Harvest Season

- Peak earning years, growing responsibilities
- Balance between growth and stability
- Focus: Optimization and acceleration

Autumn (Ages 50-65): The Preparation Season

- Approaching retirement, reducing risk
- Shifting from accumulation to preservation
- Focus: Protection and transition planning

Winter (Ages 65+): The Distribution Season

- Living off investments, legacy planning
- Capital preservation is paramount
- Focus: Income generation and wealth transfer

Each season demands a different investment philosophy, risk tolerance, and strategic focus. Get your season wrong, and even perfect execution becomes perfectly useless.

SPRING: WHEN TIME IS YOUR SUPERPOWER

Maria walked into my office at 26, clutching her $5,000 inheritance like it was nitroglycerin. She was classic Spring—young, nervous, and convinced that one wrong move would ruin her financial future forever.

"I can't afford to lose this money," she whispered, her hands shaking slightly. "It's all I have."

What Maria didn't understand is that at 26, she had something more valuable than money: she had time. And time, when properly deployed, turns small amounts into fortunes.

I showed her the mathematics of Spring:

Maria's $200 Monthly Investment Projection:

- Starting at age 26: $647,000 by age 65
- Starting at age 36: $307,000 by age 65
- Starting at age 46: $131,000 by age 65

Those ten-year delays cost her $340,000 and $516,000 respectively. Time isn't just money—it's a money multiplier.

But Spring's superpower comes with a responsibility: you must plant seeds that can grow into trees. This means:

Maximum Equity Allocation: Spring investors should hold 80-90% stocks, 10-20% bonds. Your portfolio should be aggressive enough to make your grandparents nervous.

Growth Over Income: Dividend stocks feel safe, but growth stocks create wealth. You want companies that reinvest profits into expansion, not companies that pay you to wait.

International Diversification: Don't limit yourself to U.S. markets. Spring is the time to plant seeds in emerging markets that might bloom over decades.

Skills Development: Invest in yourself aggressively. Courses, certifications, conferences—anything that increases your earning power compounds faster than any stock.

SPRING CASE STUDY: THE $50 EXPERIMENT

When Maria proved too terrified to invest $200 monthly, we started with $50. Just $50 per month into a total stock market index fund.

"I spend more than that on coffee," she admitted.

"Exactly. You're trading lattes for millions."

Eighteen months later, her $50 monthly investments had grown to $1,200. But more importantly, her identity had shifted. She stopped seeing herself as "someone who doesn't invest" and started seeing herself as "someone who builds wealth."

By year three, she had increased her contribution to $300 monthly and was researching individual stocks. Spring had done its job—not just growing her money, but growing her confidence.

SUMMER: THE PEAK PERFORMANCE YEARS

At 42, Robert had reached the Summer of his wealth-building years. His construction company was generating serious revenue. His expenses were high but stable. He had maximum earning power but also maximum financial complexity.

Summer is the season of optimization—you have income to invest, but you also have mortgages, kids' education costs, and the pressure to maintain a lifestyle that reflects your success.

"I feel like I'm making good money but never getting ahead," Robert confessed during our first meeting. "There's always something—the roof needs repair, my daughter needs braces, property taxes went up. I'm earning more than my parents ever dreamed of, but I feel broke."

This is the Summer Paradox: peak earning years can become peak spending years if you're not intentional about wealth building.

The Summer Strategy: Systematic Optimization

Summer requires a more sophisticated approach than Spring's "invest everything in growth stocks" strategy:

Asset Allocation: 70% Stocks, 30% Bonds Still growth-focused, but with enough stability to sleep at night when markets get volatile.

Tax Optimization: Summer earners hit higher tax brackets, making tax-advantaged accounts crucial:

- Max out 401(k) contributions: $23,000 annually (2024)
- Backdoor Roth IRA conversions if income limits apply
- HSA contributions: the triple-tax-advantaged account
- Consider municipal bonds if in high tax brackets

Estate Planning Foundation: Summer is when you start having assets worth protecting and meaningful family responsibilities.

Insurance Evaluation: Life and disability insurance become critical when others depend on your income.

Real Estate Strategy: Summer is often when people buy their primary residence and consider investment properties.

Estate Planning Foundation: When Success Creates Responsibility

Summer brings a new reality: you now have wealth worth protecting and people counting on your financial decisions. This is when estate planning shifts from "someday" to "this year."

Why Summer Demands Estate Planning Attention

Growing Asset Complexity: What started as simple investment accounts has evolved into business ownership, real estate holdings, and retirement accounts across multiple institutions.

Family Protection Needs: Your income supports your family's lifestyle and future plans. Estate planning ensures these needs are met regardless of what happens to you.

Peak Liability Exposure: Your success makes you a potential target for lawsuits. Proper planning includes asset protection strategies.

Tax Planning Opportunities: Summer earners benefit most from sophisticated estate and gift tax strategies.

THE SUMMER ESTATE PLANNING ESSENTIALS

Foundation Documents (Priority 1)

- Updated will with guardian nominations for children
- Durable powers of attorney for financial and healthcare decisions
- Current beneficiary designations on all accounts

- Basic asset protection review

Optimization Strategies (Priority 2)

- Life insurance evaluation for income replacement needs
- Consider revocable living trust if estate exceeds $1 million
- Coordinate estate planning with tax optimization
- Begin family conversations about values and inheritance

Advanced Planning (Priority 3)

- Business succession planning if you own a company
- Educational funding trusts for children
- Charitable giving strategies aligned with tax benefits
- Multi-generational wealth transfer planning

The key insight: Summer estate planning is about building the foundation that Autumn will optimize, and Winter will execute.

Action Step: Schedule estate planning consultation this quarter. Your growing wealth demands growing protection.

Summer Case Study: The Invisible Wealth Strategy

Robert's breakthrough came when we implemented what I call the "Invisible Wealth Strategy"—systematically redirecting money he was already spending into wealth-building vehicles.

Instead of struggling to find "extra" money to invest, we found money he was already using inefficiently:

- **Tax Savings:** Maxing his 401(k) saved $8,280 in taxes annually (at his 24% bracket)
- **Insurance Optimization:** Switching carriers saved $1,800 yearly
- **Mortgage Refi:** Lower rate saved $3,600 annually
- **Business Tax Strategies:** S-Corp election saved $4,200 in self-employment taxes

Total redirected to investments: $17,880 annually, without changing his lifestyle one bit.

"I thought building wealth meant living like a monk," Robert told me a year later. "Instead, I'm living the same way but becoming rich in the background."

AUTUMN: THE WISDOM SEASON

At 55, Sarah faced the classic Autumn dilemma. She had built a successful medical practice and accumulated $1.2 million in retirement accounts. But retirement was approaching, and her aggressive investment portfolio was starting to feel like a rollercoaster she wanted to exit.

"I keep reading about market crashes and recessions," she said during our consultation. "What if everything I've built disappears right when I need it most?"

Autumn is the season of transition—from accumulation to preservation, from growth to income, from taking risks to protecting what you've built.

The Autumn Mindset Shift

The psychological challenge of Autumn is letting go of the growth strategies that got you here. Spring and Summer were about planting and harvesting. Autumn is about storing what you've harvested for the Winter ahead.

Asset Allocation: Follow **60% Stocks, 40% Bonds** to participate in market growth, but with much more stability.

Sequence of Returns Risk: The danger in Autumn isn't just market volatility—it's experiencing major losses right before or early in retirement. A 30% loss at age 62 is devastating in a way that the same loss at age 32 was actually beneficial.

Income Planning: Start building the infrastructure for retirement income:

- Dividend-focused stock allocation
- Bond ladders for predictable income
- Cash reserves for market volatility
- Part-time work or consulting opportunities

Healthcare Considerations: Medical expenses typically increase in Autumn and explode in Winter. Plan accordingly.

Estate Planning Optimization: Advanced trust structures, tax-efficient wealth transfer strategies, and comprehensive legacy planning become critical as retirement approaches.

Autumn Case Study: The Glide Path Strategy

Sarah's portfolio transformation followed what we call a "glide path"—gradually shifting from growth to income over a five-year period:

Year 1 (Age 55): 70% stocks, 30% bonds

Year 2 (Age 56): 68% stocks, 32% bonds

Year 3 (Age 57): 65% stocks, 35% bonds

Year 4 (Age 58): 62% stocks, 38% bonds

Year 5 (Age 59): 60% stocks, 40% bonds

This gradual transition allowed her to participate in market growth while steadily reducing risk. By age 60, her portfolio was generating $48,000 annually in dividends and interest—enough to cover her basic expenses even if she never touched principal.

"I sleep better now," Sarah told me at our recent review. "Not because I have less money at risk, but because I have a plan that makes sense for where I am in life."

WINTER: THE DISTRIBUTION YEARS

James, the retired postal worker with a $1.7 million portfolio, represents Winter done right. At 68, he wasn't worried about growing his wealth—he was focused on making it last and leaving a legacy.

"I don't need to get rich anymore," he said with a smile during our annual review. "I just need to stay rich and help my grandkids get started."

Winter investing is about income generation, capital preservation, and wealth transfer. The strategies that work here would have been disastrous in Spring.

Asset Allocation: 50% Stocks, 50% Bonds/Cash to ensure enough equity exposure to fight inflation and have enough fixed income to provide stability.

The 4% Rule (With Modern Adjustments): Traditional wisdom suggests withdrawing 4% of your portfolio annually. Modern research suggests a more flexible approach:

- 3.5% in expensive market environments
- 4.5% in cheap market environments
- Adjust annually based on portfolio performance

Income-First Investing: Focus on investments that generate income naturally:

- Dividend growth stocks
- Real Estate Investment Trusts (REITs)
- Bond ladders
- Immediate or deferred annuities for guaranteed income

Legacy Execution: Winter is when comprehensive estate planning strategies get executed through systematic wealth transfer to the next generation.

Winter Case Study: The Income Machine

James's portfolio was designed as an income-generating machine:

Dividend Stocks (30%): High-quality companies with 20+ year track records of increasing dividends

REITs (10%): Real estate investment trusts providing inflation protection and income

Bond Ladder (35%): Certificates of deposit and Treasury bonds providing predictable income

Cash (15%): High-yield savings for flexibility and opportunities

Immediate Annuity (10%): Guaranteed income that covers basic expenses

This allocation generated significant income—more than his postal service pension and Social Security combined. He was able to leave principal untouched while living comfortably.

"The money works harder than I ever did," James chuckled. "And it never needs a vacation."

THE SEASONAL TRANSITION MISTAKES THAT DESTROY WEALTH

Most wealth destruction happens during seasonal transitions, which is often when people apply the wrong strategies to their current life stage:

Spring Mistakes

- Being too conservative (holding too much cash or bonds)
- Trying to time the market instead of investing consistently
- Focusing on income instead of growth
- Not investing at all due to perfectionism

Summer Mistakes

- Lifestyle inflation that consumes all income growth
- Ignoring tax optimization strategies

- Not maxing out retirement account contributions
- Buying too much house or too expensive cars
- Delaying estate planning foundation

Autumn Mistakes

- Staying too aggressive too long
- Not planning for sequence of returns risk
- Ignoring comprehensive estate planning and legacy strategies
- Panicking and becoming too conservative too quickly

Winter Mistakes

- Withdrawing too much too early
- Not having an income-focused strategy
- Leaving money in wrong account types for tax efficiency
- Not executing planned wealth transfer strategies

THE MARKET CRISIS SEASON TEST

Robert's panic call during the 2020 crash illustrates why understanding your season is crucial during market turbulence. His reaction should have been different based on his season:

If Robert was Spring (Age 28): «Buy more. This is a sale on future wealth.»

If Robert was Summer (Age 42): «Stay the course. Rebalance if needed. This is why we have bonds.»

If Robert was Autumn (Age 58): «Protect what we've built. Consider moving closer to our target allocation.»

If Robert was Winter (Age 68): «Focus on income. We have enough cash to ride this out without selling.»

Robert was actually in late Summer, approaching Autumn. The correct advice was to rebalance his portfolio to slightly more conservative allocation while staying invested for long-term growth.

He followed the plan. Eighteen months later, his portfolio had not only recovered but reached new highs. He learned that his season dictated his strategy, not his emotions.

SEASONAL REBALANCING: THE ANNUAL CHECKUP

Just as you might adjust your wardrobe for changing weather, your portfolio needs seasonal adjustments:

Annual Questions

1. Has my life situation changed enough to shift seasons?
2. Is my risk tolerance the same as last year?
3. Does my portfolio allocation match my current season?
4. What major life changes are coming that might affect my strategy?

Gradual Transitions: Don't jump from Spring to Winter overnight. Move gradually between seasons, adjusting allocation by 5-10% annually rather than making dramatic shifts.

THE COMPOUND EFFECT OF SEASONAL INVESTING

When you align your investment strategy with your life stage, magical things happen:

- You take appropriate risks when you can afford them
- You protect wealth when you need to preserve it
- You sleep better because your strategy matches your situation
- You avoid the emotional mistakes that destroy long-term wealth
- You optimize for the right outcomes at the right time

YOUR NEXT SEASONAL ACTION STEP

Based on your seasonal assessment:

If you're in Spring: Open an investment account this week and automate $100 monthly into a total stock market index fund.

If you're in Summer: Review your 401(k) allocation and increase your contribution by 2%. Schedule an estate planning consultation this quarter.

If you're in Autumn: Schedule a comprehensive portfolio review and begin comprehensive estate planning optimization.

If you're in Winter: Evaluate whether your portfolio is generating enough income to support your lifestyle without depleting principal.

Remember: there is no universal "best" investment strategy. There is only the best strategy for your current season of life.

The weather changes. Your strategy should too.

CHAPTER 5

The Five Immutable Laws of Wealth

"Ignore these five laws at your peril —wealth obeys rules, not wishes."

THE CRISIS THAT REVEALED EVERYTHING

At 3:17 AM on March 16, 2020, my phone exploded with notifications. The stock market had triggered circuit breakers, showing that oil prices had gone negative. The financial world was melting down in real-time.

But the most urgent message wasn't about markets—it was from my client David, a successful restaurant owner whose life savings had just evaporated:

"Manny, I'm ruined. Restaurants closed indefinitely. Stock portfolio down 40%. Cash reserves will last maybe 60 days. I violated every rule you taught me, didn't I?"

David had built a thriving chain of casual dining restaurants. On paper, he was wealthy since he had a $2.3 million net worth, multiple properties, and a business that generated six figures monthly. But when the pandemic hit, he discovered the difference between looking rich and being financially strong. The crisis revealed the brutal truth that, **wealth that can disappear overnight was never real wealth to begin with.**

As I sat in my home office, watching portfolios hemorrhage value while my phone buzzed with panicked clients, I realized something profound. The people who were sleeping soundly weren't the ones with the most money. They were the ones who had built their wealth on immutable laws that worked regardless of external circumstances.

David had money. But he didn't have wealth architecture.

That night, I wrote down five principles that had allowed some clients to thrive while others barely survived. These weren't strategies or tactics—they were laws as reliable as gravity and as powerful as compound interest.

LAW #1: TIME TRUMPS TIMING EVERY TIME

"Compound interest is the eighth wonder of the world. He who understands it, earns it. He who doesn't, pays it."
- Albert Einstein

The most expensive words in the English language are "I'll start investing when..."

You can come up with every excuse, "I'll do it when the market is lower, when I have more money, when I understand it better, or when the timing is perfect."

"Perfect timing" is the enemy of wealth building. Time in the market beats timing the market with mathematical certainty.

The Tale of Two Teachers

Let me tell you about Lisa and Jennifer, both teachers who started their careers at age 25 with identical $40,000 salaries.

Lisa, the Early Starter: Began investing $200 monthly at age 25. Invested for 10 years, then stopped completely. Total invested: $24,000.

Jennifer, the Waitress: Started investing $200 monthly at age 35 and continued for 30 years until retirement. Total invested: $72,000.

At age 65, assuming 8% annual returns:

- Lisa's portfolio: $314,000
- Jennifer's portfolio: $279,000

Lisa invested $48,000 less but ended up with $35,000 more. Those ten extra years of compound growth were worth more than two decades of additional contributions.

THE POWER OF STARTING IMPERFECTLY

Maria, the 26-year-old teacher from earlier chapters, exemplifies this law perfectly. She was terrified to start investing because she "didn't know enough" and "didn't have enough money."

We started her with $50 monthly despite her protest that "it isn't enough to matter."

Three years later:

- Principal invested: $1,800
- Account value: $2,247
- More importantly: transformed identity from "non-investor" to "wealth builder"

The amount didn't matter. The habit mattered. The time in the market mattered.

TIME DIVERSIFICATION: YOUR RISK REDUCTION SUPERPOWER

Young investors worry about losing money over one year. Wise investors focus on gaining wealth over decades.

Historical U.S. Stock Market Performance:

- 1-year periods: Positive returns 73% of the time
- 5-year periods: Positive returns 88% of the time
- 10-year periods: Positive returns 94% of the time
- 20-year periods: Positive returns 100% of the time

Time doesn't eliminate investment risk, but it diversifies it across decades. The longer your timeline, the more volatility becomes your friend instead of your enemy.

THE EINSTEIN IMPLEMENTATION PROTOCOL

Make compound interest your employee, not your master.

For Savers: Every $1,000 invested at age 25 becomes $21,725 by age 65 (assuming 8% returns). That's a 2,073% return on investment.

For Debtors: Every $1,000 in credit card debt at 18% interest becomes $37,000 if you only make minimum payments over 20 years. Compound interest working against you.

Action Step: Open an investment account today. Start with any amount. The best time to plant a tree was 20 years ago. The second-best time is now.

LAW #2: DISCIPLINE DEFEATS BRILLIANCE EVERY SINGLE TIME

"It's not about how much money you make. It's about how much money you keep, how hard it works for you, and how many generations you keep it for."
- Robert Kiyosaki

Wall Street wants you to believe that successful investing requires genius-level intelligence, secret information, or complex strategies. This is marketing, not mathematics.

The most successful investor in history, Warren Buffett, built his fortune using strategies a fifth grader could understand: buy good companies, hold them forever, ignore market noise.

The Millionaire Mailman Revisited

James, the postal worker who built $1.7 million on a $65,000 salary, never:

- Studied financial statements
- Timed market entries or exits
- Chased hot stock tips

- Used complex trading strategies
- Checked his portfolio daily

He simply bought dividend-growing companies every month for 30 years. His "secret" was having no secrets, instead relentless discipline applied to boring strategies.

The Discipline Stack

Discipline isn't willpower—it's system design. Build these habits in order:

Level 1: Automation Discipline
Remove emotions from the equation. Set up automatic transfers so money moves to investments before you can spend it.

Level 2: Consistency Discipline
Invest the same amount every month regardless of market conditions, personal feelings, or financial news headlines.

Level 3: Patience Discipline
Measure progress in years, not months. Ignore daily market movements. Focus on long-term wealth accumulation.

Level 4: Rebalancing Discipline
When your portfolio drifts from target allocation, mechanically rebalance. This forces you to sell high and buy low.

Level 5: Behavioral Discipline
Recognize and counter your psychological biases. Have written investment rules and follow them even when emotions scream otherwise.

THE BRILLIANT FAILURE CASE STUDY

I once worked with a client named Marcus, a brilliant software engineer who could analyze companies better than most Wall Street analysts. He had spreadsheets tracking hundreds of metrics, complex models predicting stock movements, and algorithms for optimizing entry points.

His ten-year portfolio return: 3.2% annually.

Meanwhile, his wife Sarah invested in simple index funds without any analysis. Her ten-year return: 9.7% annually.

Marcus's brilliance became his enemy. He overthought every decision, waited for perfect entry points that never came, and constantly second-guessed his choices.

Sarah's "ignorance" was her advantage. She bought the entire market every month and ignored the noise.

The 80/20 of Investment Success

80% of investment success comes from:

- Starting early (20% of factors)
- Investing consistently (20% of factors)
- Keeping costs low (20% of factors)
- Staying invested long-term (20% of factors)

20% comes from everything else Wall Street wants to sell you.

LAW #3: DIVERSIFICATION IS YOUR ONLY FREE LUNCH

"Don't put all your eggs in one basket, but don't put so few eggs in each basket that it doesn't matter if one breaks."
- Anonymous

In March 2000, a client named Paul had $500,000 invested entirely in technology stocks. "Tech is the future," he insisted. "Why would I invest in anything else?"

By October 2002, his portfolio was worth $78,000. An 84% loss that took him fifteen years to recover from.

Paul learned the most expensive lesson in investing: **concentration builds wealth, but diversification preserves it.**

THE MATHEMATICS OF DIVERSIFICATION

When you own just one stock, your portfolio moves exactly as that stock moves. Own two uncorrelated stocks, and you reduce volatility by approximately 29%. Own ten uncorrelated stocks, and volatility drops by 68%.

But here's the magic: while reducing risk through diversification, you don't significantly reduce expected returns. It's the only free lunch in investing.

Geographic Diversification: The Global Perspective

U.S. investors often suffer from "home country bias", which is overweighing domestic investments. But the U.S. represents only about 60% of global stock market value.

International Performance Comparison (Annual Returns):

- 1970s: International outperformed U.S. by 3.2%
- 1980s: U.S. outperformed International by 8.1%
- 1990s: U.S. outperformed International by 6.7%
- 2000s: International outperformed U.S. by 2.4%
- 2010s: U.S. outperformed International by 5.9%

No one can predict which will outperform in any given decade. The simple solution: own both.

Asset Class Diversification: Beyond Stocks and Bonds

Modern diversification extends beyond traditional asset classes:

Core Holdings (80%)

- U.S. Total Stock Market: 40%
- International Developed Markets: 20%
- Emerging Markets: 10%
- U.S. Bonds: 10%

Satellite Holdings (20%)

- Real Estate Investment Trusts (REITs): 10%
- Commodities: 5%
- Treasury Inflation-Protected Securities (TIPS): 5%

TIME DIVERSIFICATION: DOLLAR-COST AVERAGING

Don't just diversify across assets—diversify across time. Dollar-cost averaging means investing the same amount regularly regardless of market price.

Example: Investing $1,000 Monthly

- Month 1: Stock price $100, buy 10 shares
- Month 2: Stock price $50, buy 20 shares
- Month 3: Stock price $75, buy 13.33 shares

While the average price paid was $75 and the average market price was also $75, you own more shares purchased at lower prices, improving your position.

The Rebalancing Advantage

Diversification only works if you rebalance regularly. This forces you to sell assets that have performed well and buy assets that have performed poorly, allowing you to practice the essence of buying low and selling high.

Rebalancing Triggers

- Time-based: Quarterly or annually
- Threshold-based: When any asset class drifts 5% from target
- Combination: Check quarterly, rebalance if thresholds exceeded

LAW #4: KNOW YOUR "WHY" BEFORE YOUR "HOW"

"He who has a why to live can bear almost any how."
- Friedrich Nietzsche

David, the restaurant owner from the opening, had built wealth without purpose. He accumulated money because that is what he believed successful people did, not because he had clear reasons for building wealth.

When crisis hit, he had no emotional anchor to keep him invested for the long term. Without a compelling "why," every market downturn felt like a reason to abandon his strategy.

THE PURPOSE-DRIVEN PORTFOLIO

Compare these two approaches:

Investor A: «I want to have a million dollars because that sounds like a lot.»

Investor B: «I want to accumulate $1.2 million so I can generate $48,000 annually in dividend income, allowing me to retire early and spend time mentoring young entrepreneurs.»

When markets crash 30%, Investor A panics and sells, while Investor B sees stocks on sale and buys more. The difference is not risk tolerance, it is the clarity of purpose.

The Five Levels of Financial "Why"

Level 1: Survival - «I don't want to be broke»

Level 2: Security - «I want to feel safe financially»

Level 3: Freedom - «I want options and flexibility»

Level 4: Impact - «I want to make a difference»

Level 5: Legacy - «I want to create lasting change»

Higher-level purposes create stronger motivation and better decision-making.

PURPOSE-DRIVEN ASSET ALLOCATION

The next step is to determine your "why", which should influence your "how":

Education Funding Goals: More conservative allocation as children approach college age

Early Retirement Goals: Higher savings rate, potentially more aggressive growth allocation

Legacy Goals: Estate planning becomes crucial, tax-efficient structures matter

Charitable Goals: Donor-advised funds, charitable remainder trusts

Business Goals: More liquidity for opportunities, potentially concentrated positions

THE VALUES-BASED INVESTING MOVEMENT

Increasingly, investors want portfolios that reflect their values.

- **ESG Investing:** Environmental, Social, and Governance factors
- **Impact Investing:** Investments intended to generate positive social/environmental impact

- **Shariah-Compliant Investing:** Avoiding interest, gambling, alcohol, tobacco
- **Faith-Based Investing:** Aligning investments with religious principles

Performance doesn't require sacrificing principles. Many values-based strategies match or exceed traditional benchmark returns.

LAW #5: PROTECT WHAT YOU BUILD

"It's not how much money you make, but how much money you keep, how hard it works for you, and how many generations you keep it for."
- Robert Kiyosaki

The final law is often the most ignored: wealth without protection is just temporary abundance.

THE PROTECTION STACK

Build these defenses in order:

Layer 1: Emergency Fund

- 3-12 months of expenses in cash, depending on job stability and family situation.

Layer 2: Insurance

- Health insurance (most important)
- Life insurance (if others depend on your income)
- Disability insurance (protect your ability to earn)

- Property insurance (protect major assets)
- Umbrella liability (protect against lawsuits)

Layer 3: Legal Structure

- Will and testament
- Power of attorney (financial and healthcare)
- Beneficiary designations on all accounts
- Trust structures if appropriate

Layer 4: Tax Protection

- Maximize tax-advantaged accounts
- Tax-loss harvesting
- Asset location optimization
- Estate tax planning

Layer 5: Asset Protection

- Business entity structures
- Domestic and offshore trusts
- Homestead exemptions
- Professional liability protection

THE LAWSUIT THAT CHANGED EVERYTHING

Dr. Patricia Williams had built a successful medical practice and accumulated $3.2 million in investment accounts. She thought she was financially secure.

Then came the malpractice lawsuit. Despite having insurance, the settlement exceeded her coverage by $800,000 and because her assets weren't properly protected, she lost her home, retirement accounts, and had to start rebuilding wealth at age 52.

"I spent twenty years building wealth and five minutes losing it," she told me. "I never thought about protection until I needed it."

THE INTEGRATION OF ALL FIVE LAWS

These laws work synergistically:

Time + Discipline = Compound growth over decades

Diversification + Purpose = Appropriate risk-taking aligned with goals

Protection + Time = Sustainable wealth that survives crises

David, the restaurant owner, eventually rebuilt his wealth using all five laws:

1. **Time:** Restarted investing immediately despite losses
2. **Discipline:** Automated investments to remove emotions
3. **Diversification:** Spread risk across asset classes and geographies
4. **Purpose:** Clarified his goal of funding children's education and early retirement

5. **Protection:** Built proper insurance coverage and emergency reserves

Two years after his crisis, his net worth exceeded pre-pandemic levels. More importantly, he was finally he was wealthy *and* financially antifragile.

YOUR FIVE LAWS IMPLEMENTATION CHECKLIST

LAW #1 - TIME

- Open investment account within 7 days
- Set up automatic monthly contributions
- Choose target date fund or simple three-fund portfolio

LAW #2 - DISCIPLINE

- Write your investment policy statement
- Automate all investment contributions
- Commit to annual (not daily) portfolio reviews

LAW #3 - DIVERSIFICATION

- Ensure you own at least 1,000 stocks across multiple countries
- Include bonds appropriate for your age
- Consider real estate and commodity exposure

LAW #4 - PURPOSE

- Write down your specific financial goals
- Calculate how much you need to achieve them
- Connect investments to personal values and timeline

LAW #5 – PROTECTION

- Build emergency fund appropriate for your situation
- Review insurance coverage annually
- Update estate documents and beneficiaries
- Consider asset protection strategies

THE LAWS VS. THE NOISE

Financial media, investment salespeople, and market gurus will constantly try to convince you that success requires:

- Complex strategies
- Perfect timing
- Secret information
- Expensive products
- Constant activity

The laws say otherwise. Wealth building is simple, but not easy. It requires discipline, not brilliance. Time, not timing.

The five laws have created more millionaires than every get-rich-quick scheme combined. They've worked for centuries and will work for centuries more.

The only question is: Will you follow them?

CHAPTER 6

Investment Architecture Building Your Wealth Machine

"Build your wealth machine with precision, or watch it crumble in chaos."

THE PORTFOLIO THAT SURVIVED EVERYTHING

In February 2008, my client, Elena, sat across from my desk with the peculiar problem that she was bored with her investments.

"My portfolio just sits there," she complained. "It's not exciting. I read about people making fortunes in real estate flips and cryptocurrency. Maybe I should try something more interesting."

Elena's "boring" portfolio consisted of low-cost index funds across different asset classes. It had generated steady 8% annual returns for five years. She wanted action, but I wanted her to understand something crucial: **the best investment portfolios are designed to be boring on the outside, but revolutionary on the inside.**

Six months later, Lehman Brothers collapsed. The housing market imploded. The stock market lost 37% of its value. Millions of "exciting" portfolios evaporated.

Elena's boring portfolio? It dropped 22% and recovered within 18 months. Her portfolio continued its steady march toward her retirement goals. By 2020, her initial $100,000 had grown to $387,000.

"I'm grateful for boring," she told me during our recent review. "Boring made me rich."

That crisis taught me everything about investment architecture: **the goal is not to build a portfolio that performs spectacularly in good times, it is to build one that survives bad times and compounds wealth over decades.**

THE ARCHITECTURE METAPHOR: BUILDING FOR CENTURIES

Think of your investment portfolio like designing a building. You have three choices:

The Tent: Quick to set up, portable, exciting. Collapses in the first storm.

The House: Solid, comfortable, built for decades. Survives most weather but might struggle in extreme conditions.

The Cathedral: Designed to last centuries. Built with careful planning, quality materials, and timeless principles. Weathers every storm and becomes more beautiful with age.

Most investors build tents. Some build houses. *Wealth builders construct cathedrals.*

FOUNDATION LAYER: THE CORE PORTFOLIO

Every cathedral needs a foundation that will support everything built on top of it. In investing, this foundation consists of broad market index funds that capture the growth of entire economies.

The Three-Fund Portfolio Foundation

- **Total Stock Market Index (60%):** Owns pieces of every publicly traded U.S. company
- **International Stock Index (20%):** Owns pieces of companies around the world
- **Bond Market Index (20%):** Provides stability and income

This foundation is spectacularly boring and spectacularly effective. It requires no stock picking, no market timing, no complex analysis. It simply captures the growth of human productivity and ingenuity.

WHY INDEX FUNDS DOMINATE

Let me share a statistic that should end every debate about active vs. passive investing:

Over the past 20 years, 95% of actively managed funds failed to beat their benchmark index after accounting for fees.

Translation: If you lined up 100 professional money managers with teams of analysts, who have decades of experience and sophisticated tools, 95 of them would lose to a simple index fund that requires no human decision-making.

THE MATHEMATICS OF MEDIOCRITY

This is not about intelligence, instead it is about mathematics. Here is why index funds are nearly impossible to beat consistently:

Cost Advantage: Average actively managed fund charges 1.0% annually. Average index fund charges 0.05% annually. Over 30 years, that 0.95% difference costs $196,000 on a $100,000 investment.

Market Efficiency: In developed markets, prices already reflect most available information. «Beating the market» requires either better information, which is often illegal, or better luck, which is not sustainable.

Behavioral Advantage: Active managers face pressure to show quarterly results, leading to short-term thinking. Index funds can ignore quarterly noise and capture long-term growth.

CAPITAL ALLOCATION LAYER: RISK AND RETURN OPTIMIZATION

Once you have a solid foundation, the next layer involves optimizing your risk-return profile based on your personal situation.

The Risk-Return Relationship

This is the fundamental law of investing: higher expected returns come with higher volatility. You cannot have one without the other. Anyone promising high returns with low risk is either deluded or lying.

Asset Class Expected Returns (Historical Long-Term Averages)

- Cash: 1-2% (very low risk)
- Bonds: 4-5% (low to moderate risk)
- Real Estate: 6-7% (moderate risk)
- Stocks: 8-10% (high risk)

Risk Tolerance vs. Risk Capacity

These are different concepts often confused:

Risk Tolerance: How much volatility you can psychologically handle?

Risk Capacity: How much volatility you can financially afford?

A 25-year-old might have low risk tolerance and gets nervous about losses, but also have a high-risk capacity since they have more than forty years until retirement. A 65-year-old might have high risk tolerance and not panic about losses, but have low risk capacity since they may have more expensive lifestyle maintenance.

Optimal portfolios balance both factors.

AGE-APPROPRIATE ASSET ALLOCATION

A simple rule of thumb: your bond allocation should roughly equal your age. A 30-year-old might hold 30% bonds, 70% stocks. A 60-year-old might hold 60% bonds, 40% stocks.

But this rule has become outdated as life expectancies increase.

Modern guidelines:

Age 20-35: 10-20% bonds, 80-90% stocks

Age 35-50: 20-40% bonds, 60-80% stocks

Age 50-65: 30-50% bonds, 50-70% stocks

Age 65+: 40-60% bonds, 40-60% stocks

GEOGRAPHIC DIVERSIFICATION LAYER: GLOBAL OPTIMIZATION

U.S. investors often suffer from "home country bias", meaning they dramatically overweigh domestic investments. This creates unnecessary concentration risk.

Market Capitalization
(of global stock market) **by Country**

- United States: ~60%
- Japan: ~7%
- China: ~4%
- United Kingdom: ~4%
- Rest of World: ~25%

A globally diversified portfolio should roughly match these weights, not overweight any single country.

International Diversification Benefits

Different countries' economies do not move in perfect sync. When U.S. stocks struggle, international stocks may thrive, and vice versa.

Decade Performance Comparison

- 1970s: International outperformed U.S. by 3.8% annually
- 1980s: U.S. outperformed International by 6.1% annually
- 1990s: U.S. outperformed International by 4.2% annually
- 2000s: International outperformed U.S. by 1.6% annually
- 2010s: U.S. outperformed International by 5.3% annually

No one can predict which will outperform in the next decade. Owning both reduces timing risk.

CURRENCY DIVERSIFICATION

International investments also provide currency diversification. If the U.S. dollar weakens, foreign investments will become more valuable when converted to dollars.

Sector and Style Diversification Layer: Beyond Market Capitalization

The foundation captures entire markets, but you can enhance returns by tilting toward factors that have historically outperformed.

Factor Investing: The Academic Approach

Decades of academic research have identified factors that explain most investment returns:

- **Size Factor:** Small-cap stocks have historically outperformed large-cap stocks
- **Value Factor:** Cheap stocks have historically outperformed expensive stocks
- **Profitability Factor:** Profitable companies outperform unprofitable ones
- **Investment Factor:** Companies that invest conservatively outperform those that over-invest
- **Implementation Through Factor Tilts**

You can capture these premiums by tilting your portfolio:

- **Core U.S. Stocks (40%):** Total Stock Market Index
- **International Developed (15%):** Broad international exposure
- **Bonds (10%):** Government and corporate bonds
- **U.S. Small-Cap Value (10%):** Small companies trading at low valuations
- **U.S. Large-Cap Value (10%):** Large companies trading at low valuations
- **International Small-Cap (5%):** Small international companies
- **Emerging Markets (5%):** Developing country exposure
- **REITs (5%):** Real estate investment trusts

REBALANCING LAYER: THE DISCIPLINE ADVANTAGE

The most important part of portfolio management is not choosing investments — it is maintaining discipline through rebalancing.

Rebalancing Forces Good Behavior

When you rebalance, you will:

- Sell high, meaning, sell assets that have performed well
- Buy low, meaning you buy assets that have performed poorly
- Maintain your target risk level
- Remove emotions from investment decisions

Rebalancing Triggers

It is crucial to know the "triggers" that will let you know when to rebalance.

Time-Based: Rebalance quarterly or annually regardless of market movements

Threshold-Based: Rebalance when any asset class drifts more than 5% from target allocation

Combination Approach: Check allocations quarterly, rebalance only when thresholds are exceeded

THE REBALANCING BONUS

Studies show that disciplined rebalancing adds 0.35% to 0.45% annually to portfolio returns. This "rebalancing bonus" comes from consistently buying low and selling high.

Tax Optimization Layer: Keeping More of What You Earn

Where you hold investments matters almost as much as what you invest in.

Asset Location Strategy

Different account types have different tax characteristics:

Tax-Deferred Accounts (401k, Traditional IRA)

- Contributions reduce current taxes
- Growth is tax-deferred
- Withdrawals taxed as ordinary income
- Best for: Bonds, REITs, international funds

Tax-Free Accounts (Roth IRA, Roth 401k)

- Contributions made with after-tax dollars
- Growth is tax-free forever
- Withdrawals tax-free in retirement
- Best for: High-growth stocks, small-cap funds

Taxable Accounts

- No contribution limits
- Investments taxed annually

- Capital gains rates lower than ordinary income
- Best for: Tax-efficient index funds, municipal bonds

Tax-Loss Harvesting

In taxable accounts, you can sell losing investments to offset gains from winning investments, reducing your tax bill.

MUNICIPAL BOND CONSIDERATION

For high earners in high-tax states, municipal bonds can provide better after-tax returns than corporate bonds.

Tax-Equivalent Yield Formula: Municipal Bond Yield ÷ (1 - Tax Rate) = Taxable Equivalent Yield

*Example: 3% municipal bond for someone in 35% tax bracket = 4.6% taxable equivalent yield

BEHAVIORAL ARCHITECTURE LAYER: DESIGNING FOR HUMAN NATURE

The final layer addresses the biggest threat to investment success: your own behavior.

The Behavior Gap

Studies consistently show that average investors earn less than their investments. How is this possible?

Investor Behavior

- Buy when markets are high (feeling optimistic)
- Sell when markets are low (feeling pessimistic)

- Chase performance (buy last year's winners)
- Panic during volatility (abandon long-term plans)

DESIGNING FOR SUCCESS

Your portfolio architecture should make good behavior easy and bad behavior difficult. Following these guidelines will keep your behavior in check.

Automatic Investing: Money moves to investments before you can spend it

Simple Allocation: Complex portfolios encourage tinkering

Clear Guidelines: Written investment policy prevents emotional decisions

Regular Reviews: Scheduled check-ins prevent daily monitoring

The Investment Policy Statement

Every serious investor needs a written investment policy statement (IPS) that includes:

- Investment goals and timeline
- Risk tolerance and capacity
- Target asset allocation
- Rebalancing guidelines
- Contribution schedule
- Review frequency

Sample Investment Policy Statement:

"My goal is to accumulate $1 million for retirement by age 65. I will contribute $500 monthly to a portfolio consisting of 70% stocks and 30% bonds. I will rebalance annually and not make changes based on market movements or financial media. I will review this policy every three years or after major life changes."

THE COMPLETE ARCHITECTURE EXAMPLE: SARAH'S CATHEDRAL PORTFOLIO

Let me show you how all these layers work together using Sarah, a 35-year-old professional earning $75,000 annually:

Foundation (80% of portfolio)

- Total Stock Market Index: 45%
- International Stock Index: 15%
- Bond Index: 20%

Enhancement Tilts (15% of portfolio)

- Small-Cap Value Index: 5%
- International Small-Cap Index: 5%
- REITs: 5%

Stability Layer (5% of portfolio)

- High-Yield Savings: 5%

Account Allocation:

- 401(k): $18,000 annually (bonds, REITs, international)

- Roth IRA: $6,000 annually (small-cap value, growth stocks)
- Taxable: $6,000 annually (total stock market index)

Rebalancing: Annual review, rebalance if any allocation drifts >5% from target

This architecture is designed to capture market returns while managing risk, minimizing taxes, and preventing behavioral mistakes.

COMMON ARCHITECTURE MISTAKES THAT DESTROY WEALTH

Below are the following mistakes that can destroy the wealth you have been working so hard towards.

Over-Diversification: Owning 50 different funds that all do the same thing increases costs and complexity, and ultimately not reducing risk.

Under-Diversification: Putting all money in a single stock, sector, or country creates unnecessary concentration risk.

Complexity Addiction: Sophisticated strategies often produce inferior results compared to simple approaches.

Performance Chasing: Constantly switching strategies based on recent performance guarantees buying high and selling low.

Fee Blindness: Ignoring investment costs that compound over decades into massive wealth transfers to financial companies.

Timing Attempts: Trying to get in and out of markets based on predictions that are right about 50% of the time.

THE ARCHITECTURE THAT BUILT MILLIONAIRES

Remember James, the postal worker who built $1.7 million? His architecture was breathtakingly simple:

Entire Portfolio:

- S&P 500 Index Fund: 70%
- Total Bond Market Index: 30%

Contributions: $500 monthly for 30 years

Rebalancing: Once annually

Behavior: Never sold, never stopped contributing, never changed strategy

Simple. Boring. Effective.

Elena, who initially wanted excitement, now has $387,000 from her "boring" portfolio. Sarah's cathedral portfolio is on track to exceed $1 million by retirement.

YOUR ARCHITECTURE BLUEPRINT

Building investment architecture requires answering these fundamental questions:

1. **What are my specific financial goals and timeline?**
2. **How much volatility can I psychologically and financially handle?**
3. **What's my tax situation and how can I optimize for it?**

4. **How can I design my portfolio to prevent behavioral mistakes?**
5. **What's the simplest approach that achieves my goals?**

Start with the foundation: a simple three-fund portfolio. Add complexity only if it serves a specific purpose and you understand the trade-offs.

Remember: you are not building a portfolio to impress people or generate excitement. You are building a wealth machine designed to compound your money for decades, while you focus on living your life.

The best architecture is the one you can stick with through bull markets, bear markets, and everything in between.

Build your cathedral. Let time and compound interest do the rest.

PART III

LEGACY—"WHY NOT US?"

CHAPTER 7

The Estate Planning Wake-Up Call

"An estate plan isn't a document
—it's your family's lifeline after you're gone."

THE PHONE CALL THAT CHANGES EVERYTHING

The call came at 11:47 PM on a Tuesday. I was in deep sleep when my phone pierced the silence with the kind of urgent buzz that means someone's world just collapsed.

"Manny?" The voice was barely recognizable—shaky, raw, desperate. "It's Patricia. Tom died tonight. Heart attack. He was only fifty-two."

Dr. Patricia Williams had been my client for three years. She and her husband, Tom, had built what seemed like an ideal life: a successful medical practice, a beautiful home in Short Hills, two children at private schools, and retirement accounts approaching seven figures. They were the picture of suburban success.

But as Patricia's voice cracked through the phone, I realized they had made a mistake that would haunt their family for decades. They had built wealth without building the systems to protect it.

"Manny, I don't know what to do. Tom handled all the money stuff. I don't even know where our accounts are. And the kids... oh God, the kids. What happens to them if something happens to me?"

In that moment, Patricia discovered the difference between having money and having financial security; the difference between accumulating wealth and architecting a legacy.

Over the next six months, I watched Patricia navigate a nightmare that could have been prevented with a few hours of planning: bank accounts frozen because they were in Tom's name only, investment accounts tied up in probate; insurance policies with outdated beneficiaries; and a will that had not been updated since their first child was born.

Tom's death taught me something I'll never forget: **The most tragic financial failures aren't caused by market crashes or bad investments. They are caused by the absence of a plan for what happens when the inevitable becomes reality.**

THE $2.3 MILLION MISTAKE

Let me tell you about another client, David Chen, a successful technology consultant that thought he had everything figured out.

David spent twenty years building a thriving business and accumulated $2.3 million in various accounts. He was proud of what he had built from nothing. He is the son of immigrants who had created generational wealth through hard work and smart decisions.

But David made one catastrophic oversight: he never created a plan for transferring that wealth to his family.

When David died suddenly at fifty-eight, the financial devastation was swift and merciless. Below, I have outlined what hurt his family financially the most.

- **Estate taxes consumed $460,000** (20% of his wealth)
- **Probate costs ate another $115,000** (legal fees, court costs, delays)
- **Family fighting over unclear intentions cost $180,000** (additional legal fees)
- **Business partnership disputes consumed $320,000** (forced liquidation)

David's family received $1.22 million of his $2.3 million estate. Almost half of his life's work disappeared into the machinery of an inefficient transfer system.

The tragedy? All of it could have been prevented with proper estate planning that would have cost less than $15,000.

THE ESTATE PLANNING PARADOX

Here is the brutal irony: the people who are most diligent about building wealth are often the least prepared for transferring it.

They will spend hours researching the perfect investment, but will not spend thirty minutes updating beneficiary designations. They will optimize their portfolio allocation to the decimal point, but have not created a will in fifteen years. They'll stress about expense ratios but will ignore the potential for 40% estate tax liability.

This isn't about intelligence or diligence. It's about human psychology. We build wealth in the present, but we plan for death in the future. And the future always feels far away, until it becomes the present.

THE THREE PILLARS OF LEGACY ARCHITECTURE

After helping hundreds of families navigate wealth transfer, I have identified three foundational elements that separate families who successfully preserve wealth from those who lose it:

Pillar 1, Legal Architecture: Documents and structures that control how wealth moves when you can't control it yourself.

Pillar 2, Tax Optimization: Strategies that minimize the government's claim on your wealth during transfer.

Pillar 3, Family Preparation: Systems that prepare the next generation to receive, manage, and multiply inherited wealth.

Most families focus exclusively on Pillar 1, ignore Pillar 2, and completely neglect Pillar 3. This imbalance explains why the majority of wealthy families lose their wealth by the second generation.

PILLAR 1: LEGAL ARCHITECTURE - YOUR WEALTH'S FOUNDATION

The legal architecture of wealth transfer consists of documents and structures that ensure your wealth goes where, when, and how you want it to go.

The Essential Documents

Last Will and Testament are your "final instructions". Your will is the document that speaks for you when you cannot speak for yourself.

Yet 60% of Americans do not have one, including many wealthy individuals who should know better.

What a Will Controls:

- Distribution of assets not covered by other documents
- Guardianship of minor children
- Executor appointment and powers
- Personal property distribution
- Charitable bequests

What a Will Cannot Control:

- Assets with beneficiary designations (401k, IRA, life insurance)
- Jointly owned property
- Trust assets
- Assets with transfer-on-death designations

THE WILL VS. TRUST DECISION MATRIX

Use a Will When:

- Estate value under $1 million
- Simple family structure
- No minor children or special needs beneficiaries

- No privacy concerns
- Cost is primary consideration

Use a Trust When:

- Estate value over $1 million
- Complex family dynamics
- Minor children or beneficiaries with special needs
- Privacy is important
- Want to avoid probate delays and costs

REVOCABLE LIVING TRUSTS: YOUR ESTATE PLANNING SWISS ARMY KNIFE

A revocable living trust is like creating a corporation for your personal wealth. You remain in complete control during your lifetime, but the trust provides structure for management and distribution after your death.

Trust Benefits:

- **Probate Avoidance:** Assets transfer immediately to beneficiaries
- **Privacy Protection:** Trust terms remain confidential
- **Incapacity Planning:** Successor trustee manages assets if you become unable
- **Flexibility:** Can be modified or revoked during lifetime

- **Professional Management:** Can specify investment management for beneficiaries

Trust Drawbacks:

- **Higher Cost:** $3,000-$8,000 vs. $500-$1,500 for will
- **Maintenance Required:** Must transfer assets into trust
- **Complexity:** More complicated than simple will

POWERS OF ATTORNEY: YOUR FINANCIAL AND MEDICAL DEPUTIES

Powers of attorney is one of the most important documents that most people do not understand.

Financial Power of Attorney: Authorizes someone to make financial decisions on your behalf if you become incapacitated. Without this document, your family would need court approval to access your accounts or pay your bills.

Healthcare Power of Attorney: Authorizes someone to make medical decisions on your behalf if you're unable to do so. This includes decisions about life support, treatment options, and end-of-life care.

THE INCAPACITY CRISIS

Consider this scenario: You are in a coma after a car accident. Your spouse needs to access your individual retirement account to pay for medical care. Without a proper financial power of attorney, your spouse would need to:

1. Hire an attorney
2. File for conservatorship in court
3. Wait 3-6 months for court approval
4. Pay ongoing court supervision fees
5. File annual reports with the court

Meanwhile, bills accumulate, and investment opportunities disappear.

HEALTHCARE DIRECTIVES: YOUR MEDICAL WISHES

Healthcare directives communicate your wishes about medical treatment when you can't communicate them yourself.

Living Will: Specifies your wishes about life-sustaining treatment in terminal situations

Healthcare Power of Attorney: Designates someone to make medical decisions for you

HIPAA Authorization: Allows designated people to access your medical information

THE TERRY SCHIAVO EFFECT

The highly publicized Terry Schiavo case in 2005 showed America what happens when families disagree about end-of-life care and are left without clear documentation. The legal battle lasted seven years, cost hundreds of thousands of dollars, and tore the family apart.

Clear healthcare directives prevent family conflicts during already traumatic situations.

BENEFICIARY DESIGNATIONS: THE OVERLOOKED WEALTH TRANSFER TOOL

Beneficiary designations might be the most powerful estate planning tool most people ignore. These simple forms override wills and trusts, allowing assets to transfer directly to named beneficiaries.

Assets with Beneficiary Designations

- 401(k) and 403(b) accounts
- Individual Retirement Accounts (IRA)
- Life insurance policies
- Bank accounts (POD - Payable on Death)
- Investment accounts (TOD - Transfer on Death)
- Annuities

THE $500,000 BENEFICIARY MISTAKE

Mark divorced his first wife fifteen years ago and remarried. He updated his will, his trust, and his insurance policies to benefit his new wife. But he forgot to change the beneficiary designation on his 401(k) account.

When Mark died, his $500,000 retirement account went to his ex-wife, despite his will stating otherwise. His current wife received nothing from his largest asset because beneficiary designations override all other documents.

BENEFICIARY DESIGNATION BEST PRACTICES

Primary and Contingent Beneficiaries: Always name backup beneficiaries in case primary beneficiaries predecease you

Specific Percentages: Use percentages rather than dollar amounts because accounts grow over time

Annual Reviews: Update beneficiaries after major life events like marriage, divorce, births, and deaths

Institutional Beneficiaries: Name a trust (not individuals) as the beneficiary when leaving money to minor children or family members who can't manage large inheritances responsibly. The trust acts as a financial guardian, controlling when and how the money gets distributed."

PILLAR 2: TAX OPTIMIZATION - KEEPING MORE FOR YOUR FAMILY

Estate taxes can consume 40% of wealth above certain thresholds. For families below certain estate tax limits, income taxes on inherited retirement accounts can be devastating.

Federal Estate Tax Landscape

2024 Federal Estate Tax Exemption: $13.61 million per person ($27.22 million for married couples)

2026 Sunset Provision: Exemption drops to approximately $7 million per person unless Congress acts

Federal Estate Tax Rate: 40% on amounts above exemption

State Estate Taxes: Twelve states, plus the District of Columbia, impose state estate taxes with much lower exemption thresholds

States with Lowest Exemptions:

- Oregon: $1 million
- Massachusetts: $2 million
- Rhode Island: $1.733 million
- Connecticut: $12.92 million

Families in these states face estate tax liability at much lower wealth levels.

INCOME TAX TIME BOMBS IN RETIREMENT ACCOUNTS

The SECURE Act of 2019 created a massive tax acceleration for inherited retirement accounts. Most non-spouse beneficiaries must now withdraw all funds within ten years, potentially pushing them into higher tax brackets.

Pre-SECURE Act: Beneficiaries could «stretch» withdrawals over their lifetime

Post-SECURE Act: Most beneficiaries must empty inherited accounts within ten years

THE $200,000 TAX ACCELERATION

Sarah inherited her father's $500,000 IRA. Under old rules, she could withdraw approximately $15,000 annually over her 40-year life expectancy, paying taxes at her normal rate.

Under new rules, she must withdraw $50,000 annually for ten years. Combined with her $80,000 salary, these withdrawals push her into higher tax brackets, increasing her tax bill by approximately $200,000 over the ten-year period.

ESTATE TAX MITIGATION STRATEGIES

Annual Exclusion Gifts: $18,000 per recipient per year (2024) can be gifted without using lifetime exemption

Lifetime Exemption Utilization: Consider making larger gifts while exemption is high

Grantor Retained Annuity Trusts (GRATs): Transfer appreciation to beneficiaries at reduced gift tax cost

Charitable Remainder Trusts: Provide income during lifetime while creating charitable deduction

Life Insurance: Create estate tax liquidity and leverage gift tax exemptions

ROTH IRA CONVERSIONS FOR LEGACY PLANNING

Converting traditional IRAs to Roth IRAs creates a powerful legacy tool:

Benefits for Heirs

- Tax-free withdrawals, including growth
- No required minimum distributions during owner's lifetime
- Ten-year withdrawal requirement still applies, but withdrawals are tax-free

Benefits for Owners

- No required minimum distributions
- Tax diversification in retirement
- Potential tax savings if done strategically

PILLAR 3: FAMILY PREPARATION, THE MOST CRITICAL ELEMENT

The most sophisticated legal and tax strategies are worthless if the next generation isn't prepared to receive, manage, and multiply inherited wealth.

THE WEALTH TRANSFER FAILURE STATISTICS

70% of wealthy families lose their wealth by the second generation, and 90% lose it by the third generation

These failures are not caused by market crashes or economic downturns. They are caused by:

- Lack of financial education
- Absence of shared family values
- Poor communication about wealth
- Entitlement and lack of purpose
- Family conflicts and litigation

THE PREPARATION FRAMEWORK

Phase 1: Financial Education (Ages 8-18) Age-appropriate education about money, investing, and wealth stewardship

Phase 2: Responsibility Development (Ages 18-25) Opportunities to earn, manage, and lose money in controlled environments

Phase 3: Stewardship Training (Ages 25-35) Involvement in family investment decisions and charitable activities

Phase 4: Leadership Transition (Ages 35+) Gradual transition of wealth management responsibilities

FAMILY GOVERNANCE SYSTEMS

Successful multi-generational families create formal systems for decision-making, conflict resolution, and wealth management. You can build your own by creating your own…

Family Mission Statement: Written document articulating family values and wealth purpose

Family Council: Formal body that makes major family decisions

Investment Committee: Group responsible for overseeing family investments

Next Generation Board: Committee focused on developing younger family members

Conflict Resolution Process: Predetermined steps for addressing family disagreements

Communication Protocols: Regular family meetings, financial reporting, and transparency standards

THE JOHNSON FAMILY SUCCESS STORY

The Johnson family built wealth through a chain of hardware stores across three states. When the patriarch retired, he faced a common dilemma: his three children had different interests and capabilities.

Instead of simply dividing the business equally, the family created a comprehensive governance system built up by the following:

Family Constitution: Document outlining family values, decision-making processes, and participation requirements

Leadership Development Program: Mandatory business education and external work experience for all family members

Performance-Based Ownership: Equity stakes based on contribution and competence, not just bloodline

Buy-Sell Agreements: Clear processes for family members who want to exit the business

Charitable Foundation: Shared family activity that builds unity while creating positive impact

Through this work, the business has grown from 12 stores to 47 stores within three generations. Family members work together harmoniously because they have systems for making decisions and resolving conflicts.

THE INTEGRATION CHALLENGE, MAKING IT ALL WORK TOGETHER

Family preparation without legal structure leaves wealth vulnerable. The three pillars of legacy architecture must work together seamlessly. Legal documents without tax planning will leave money on the table and tax strategies without family preparation create entitled heirs. Following the guidelines I described above, will allow families to continue to grow over multi-generations.

THE ANNUAL LEGACY REVIEW PROCESS

Legal Architecture Review:

- Update documents after major life events
- Review beneficiary designations annually
- Ensure trust funding is current
- Verify powers of attorney are up to date

Tax Strategy Assessment:

- Project estate tax liability based on current wealth
- Evaluate gift tax opportunities
- Consider Roth IRA conversion strategies
- Review charitable giving plans

Family Preparation Evaluation:

- Assess next generation's financial education progress
- Evaluate family communication effectiveness

- Review governance system performance
- Plan family meetings and education activities

THE LEGACY PLANNING TIMELINE

Ages 25-35: Foundation Building

- Create basic will and powers of attorney
- Establish proper beneficiary designations
- Begin family financial education if children present
- Consider life insurance for income replacement

Ages 35-50: Wealth Accumulation Phase

- Establish trust structures if wealth exceeds $1 million
- Implement gift tax strategies
- Develop family governance systems
- Create comprehensive insurance review

Ages 50-65: Legacy Transition Phase

- Execute major gift tax strategies before sunset
- Begin leadership transition to next generation
- Establish charitable giving legacy
- Complete comprehensive estate plan review

Ages 65+: Legacy Preservation Phase

- Focus on income tax efficient wealth transfer
- Finalize family governance transition

- Complete charitable legacy planning
- Ensure all documents reflect final wishes

YOUR LEGACY PLANNING ACTION STEPS

Immediate Actions (Next 30 Days):

- Calculate your potential estate tax liability
- Review all beneficiary designations
- Schedule estate planning attorney consultation
- Begin family conversations about wealth values

Short-Term Goals (Next 6 Months):

- Complete basic estate planning documents
- Implement annual gift tax strategy
- Establish family financial education plan
- Review insurance coverage adequacy

Long-Term Objectives (Next 2 Years):

- Develop comprehensive family governance system
- Execute advanced tax planning strategies
- Create charitable giving legacy plan
- Establish next generation leadership development

THE CHOICE THAT DEFINES YOUR LEGACY

Patricia Williams learned the hard way that wealth without planning is just temporary abundance. After Tom's death, she spent two years and $75,000 in legal fees to resolve what could have been avoided with $15,000 in proactive planning.

But Patricia's story has a redemptive ending. After experiencing the chaos of unprepared wealth transfer, she became obsessed with legacy planning. She created comprehensive documents, implemented tax strategies, and began preparing her children for their inheritance responsibilities.

"I won't let another family go through what we went through," she told me recently. "Tom and I thought we were building wealth for our children. We didn't realize we were also building problems for them."

Today, Patricia's children are financially educated, values-driven, and prepared to be good stewards of their inheritance. What started as a cautionary tale became a success story through intentional planning and family preparation.

The question every wealth builder must answer: Are you building wealth for your family, or are you building problems for them?

The choice you make determines whether your legacy multiplies across generations or disappears within one.

CHAPTER 8

Raising Money-Smart Kids

"Raise kids who master money, not just inherit it —legacy starts with them."

THE CONVERSATION THAT STARTED EVERYTHING

I was sitting next to my daughter, Brooke, who was watching her favorite player at Giants Stadium. She then asked,

"Dad, are we rich?"

The question hit me like an interception when the Giants are down in the fourth quarter. She was only eleven years old but still mature enough to notice the differences between our family's lifestyle and that a few of her classmates.

I looked into her curious brown eyes and thought about how this moment would shape her relationship with money for the rest of her life. I realized how I answered this question would either open the door to financial wisdom or lock her into limiting beliefs about wealth and success.

"What do you think being rich means?" I asked, buying myself time to craft an answer that would serve her for decades.

"Rich people have lots of money and can buy whatever they want," she said, her attention split between our conversation and the action on the field.

"That's one way to think about it," I said. "But I think being rich means having choices. It means being able to decide how you spend your time, who you help, and what kind of impact you want to make in the world."

That conversation launched a financial education journey that would transform not just Brooke's understanding of money, but my own understanding of how wealth gets passed down each generation.

THE $500,000 QUESTION EVERY PARENT FACES

Here is a statistic that should terrify every parent building wealth: **Children from wealthy families are more likely to struggle with money management as adults than those from middle-class families.**

This is not about intelligence or opportunity. It is about preparation. Wealthy parents often shield their children from financial realities, believing they are protecting them from stress. Instead, they are creating adults who inherit money and not the wisdom to manage it.

Consider the math: If you have successfully built $500,000 in investable assets and pass them to a financially unprepared child, you have essentially handed them a loaded weapon. Their inheritance could launch their financial independence or destroy their financial security.

The difference is not the money—it is the education that comes with it.

THE THREE FINANCIAL PARENTING MISTAKES THAT DESTROY GENERATIONAL WEALTH

Mistake #1, The Secrecy Strategy: «We don't discuss money in front of the children.»

Parents often think they are protecting their kids by keeping financial information private. Instead, they are raising financially illiterate adults who learn about money from social media, friends, and marketing messages rather than from the people who built wealth.

Mistake #2, The Rescue Reflex: «I don't want my kids to struggle like I did.»

Parents who grew up with financial stress often overcompensate by removing all financial obstacles from their children's lives. But struggle builds resilience, decision-making skills, and appreciation for value. Remove the struggle, and you remove the education.

Mistake #3, The Delayed Disclosure: «We'll tell them about their inheritance when they're older.»

Parents postpone financial education until their children are adults, and then simultaneously dump wealth and responsibility on them. It is like waiting until someone turns eighteen to teach them to drive and then handing them the keys to a Formula One race car.

THE AGE-APPROPRIATE FINANCIAL EDUCATION FRAMEWORK

Financial education is not a single conversation; it is an ongoing curriculum that evolves with your child's development. Below,

I have created a guide specifically designed for each age group to support your child's financial literacy journey.

Ages 3-7: The Foundation Years

Core Concepts

- Money is earned through work!
- Most things cost money
- Waiting and saving allows us to buy things we want
- Sharing money helps other people

Practical Activities

1. **The Three-Jar System:** Save, Spend, Share jars for allowance allocation
2. **Store Negotiations:** Let them choose between items within a budget
3. **Work-for-Money:** Small chores tied to small payments
4. **Charity Involvement:** Let them choose where to donate their «share» money

Key Lessons

- Money is finite spending, means the money is gone
- Delayed gratification will lead to better outcomes
- Work creates value that can be exchanged for money
- Helping others is an important use of money

REAL WORLD EXAMPLE: WHEN FINANCIAL EDUCATION STARTS WITH FISHER-PRICE

The most important financial lesson I ever taught happened at a plastic kitchen set in my living room when Brooke was four years old.

"Dad, can you buy me ice cream?" she asked, holding up a toy shopping basket filled with plastic groceries.

Instead of just saying yes or no, I knelt down to her eye level and pulled out my wallet. "Let me show you something, sweetheart. See this money? When I give it to the ice cream man, I don't have it anymore. So, we need to choose ice cream today or save this money to help buy those art supplies you wanted for your room."

Her little forehead wrinkled in concentration. "If I pick ice cream, no art supplies?"

"Not no art supplies forever," I explained. "But we'd have to wait longer to save enough money for them."

She stared at the dollar bills for what felt like an eternity. Then she carefully placed them back in my wallet. "Art supplies, please. Ice cream is gone too fast."

In that moment, at four years old, Brooke learned the foundation of all wealth building.

Ages 8-12: The Building Years

Core Concepts

- Compound interest and long-term saving
- Entrepreneurship and value creation
- Smart spending vs. wasteful spending
- Basic investing principles

Practical Activities

1. **Savings Account Opening:** Real bank account with quarterly interest discussions
2. **Business Projects:** Lemonade stands, pet-sitting, lawn care businesses
3. **Comparison Shopping:** Teaching price awareness and value assessment
4. **Investment Games:** Stock picking contests with fake money

REAL-WORLD EXAMPLE: THE LAWN MOWING EVOLUTION

When Brooke turned nine, she wanted expensive art supplies for her drawing hobby. Instead of buying them outright, I proposed a partnership. She would start a lawn mowing business in our neighborhood, and I would provide the startup capital for equipment in exchange for 50% of profits until the loan was repaid.

Over that summer, Brooke learned,

- **Customer service**: Some neighbors were easier to please than others.
- **Quality control**: Rushed jobs led to complaints and reduced pay.
- **Pricing strategy**: She could charge more for excellent work.
- **Expense management**: Gas and maintenance reduced her profits.
- **Reinvestment**: Better equipment led to faster work and higher profits.

By the end of the summer, she earned enough for her art supplies, repaid the equipment loan, and had $200 in her savings account. Most importantly, she understood that money was earned, not given.

Ages 13-17: The Application Years

Core Concepts

- Credit and debt management
- Career planning and income potential
- Tax basics and financial responsibility
- Investment portfolio construction

Practical Activities

1. **Part-Time Jobs:** Real work experience with supervision and coaching
2. **Budget Management:** Monthly allowance that covers all discretionary expenses
3. **Investment Account:** Real money in a custodial investment account
4. **College Funding Participation:** Understanding education costs and funding sources

REAL WORLD EXAMPLE: THE TEACHING POWER OF REAL STAKES

At fifteen, Brooke wanted to take college visits to Florida schools. We'd fallen in love with the state during a club lacrosse tournament in Tampa, and she was excited about the possibility of playing lacrosse and studying somewhere warm. But a proper college visit trip flights, hotels, rental cars, meals, and campus tours across multiple schools would cost around $3,000.

I presented her with three options:

1. Wait until junior year when college visits become more standard

2. Take out a "family loan" and repay it through part-time work

3. Find a way to earn the money herself for the trip

She chose option three. Over six months, she doubled down on her job watching kids at the after-school program and picked up additional babysitting gigs for her club lacrosse teammates' families and neighbors. Working twenty hours per week at $15 per hour, she earned $2,100 and we contributed the remaining $900 as a "travel scholarship" for her effort.

The college visits were more meaningful because she had invested her own effort to make them happen. At each campus, when admissions counselors asked about her interest in their school, Brooke could authentically say she'd worked six months just for the opportunity to visit. That level of demonstrated commitment made a lasting impression.

She also learned that expensive opportunities—whether they are college trips, college tuition, or future career investments—are achievable through planning and work. The trip wasn't just about touring campuses; it was about understanding that the things you want most require the most effort to achieve.

When we returned to New Jersey, Brooke had a clear vision for her college goals and a proven system for earning what she needed to achieve them.

Ages 18-25: The Transition Years

Core Concepts

- Credit building and debt avoidance
- Career development and income optimization
- Tax planning and financial independence basics
- Investment strategy refinement

Practical Activities

1. **Credit Card Training:** Supervised credit card use with clear guidelines
2. **Apartment Management:** Paying rent, utilities, and living expenses to understand responsibility
3. **Investment Portfolio Management:** Gradually increasing control over investment decisions
4. **Family Financial Participation:** Observer status in family financial discussions

REAL LIFE EXAMPLE: THE FAMILY INVESTMENT COMMITTEE

Starting when Brooke turned sixteen, I invited her to join our family's quarterly investment reviews. She did not make decisions, but she participated in discussions about portfolio allocation, market conditions, and long-term strategy.

These sessions accomplish several goals:

- **Demystify Investing:** She sees that successful investing is methodical, not magical.

- **Build Confidence:** Her questions and observations are valued and discussed seriously.
- **Develop Judgment:** She learns to think long-term and ignore short-term market noise.
- **Understand Responsibility:** She sees the work required to build and maintain wealth.

TEACHING FINANCIAL VALUES, NOT JUST FINANCIAL SKILLS

Technical knowledge about investing and budgeting is important, but values drive behavior. The most financially successful families are those that develop strong values around money.

Value #1, Money is a Tool, Not a Goal: Money should amplify your ability to create value, solve problems, and help others. It's not a scorekeeping system for personal worth.

Teaching Approach: Focus conversations on what money enables rather than money itself. «This investment account will give you choices about your career.» «Our savings let us help Grandma when she needed medical care.»

Value #2, Earning Precedes Spending: Every dollar should be connected to value creation. Spending without earning leads to entitlement and poor decision-making.

Teaching Approach: Connect purchases to work, even in small ways. «You can have those shoes after you complete your lawn mowing jobs this week.» «Let's calculate how many hours of babysitting that concert ticket costs.»

Value #3, Delayed Gratification Creates Better Outcomes: The ability to postpone immediate pleasure for long-term gain is the foundation of wealth building and life success.

Teaching Approach: Create situations where waiting produces better results. «You can have one piece of candy now, or three pieces after dinner.» Or "You can spend your savings on a video game today or wait three months and buy two games."

Value #4, Sharing Creates Meaning: Wealth without purpose leads to emptiness. Teaching children to share money and time with others creates perspective and purpose.

Teaching Approach: Make charitable giving a family activity. Ask questions like, "Let's research local charities and decide where to donate this month" or "How can we use our resources to help our community?".

THE ALLOWANCE STRATEGY THAT BUILDS CHARACTER

Most families approach allowances wrong. They either tie them entirely to chores, which turns family contribution into transactional work, or give them freely, which is teaching entitlement. The best approach combines both elements strategically.

THE THREE-PART ALLOWANCE SYSTEM

Part 1: Family Contribution (40% of allowance)

- Money earned for age-appropriate family responsibilities. This teaches that everyone contributes to family success and receives compensation for their efforts.

Part 2: Base Allowance (40% of allowance)

- Money given simply for being part of the family. This teaches that families support each other and provides security for basic needs.

Part 3: Performance Bonus (20% of allowance)

- Additional money earned for exceptional effort, attitude, or results. This teaches that extraordinary effort leads to extraordinary rewards.

Allowance Implementation Example

Brooke's Age 12 Allowance: $20 weekly

- $8 for family responsibilities (feeding pets, organizing playroom, helping with yard work)
- $8 base allowance (no strings attached)
- $4 performance bonus opportunity (exceptional helpfulness, academic achievement, positive attitude)

Required Allocation:

- 30% to savings account
- 20% to charity/sharing
- 50% for discretionary spending

This system teaches earning, budgeting, saving, and sharing, while maintaining family harmony.

THE TECHNOLOGY CHALLENGE: RAISING MONEY-SMART KIDS IN A DIGITAL WORLD

Today's children face financial education challenges that did not exist for previous generations:

Digital Money Disconnection: Credit cards, Venmo, and online shopping make money abstract rather than tangible.

Instant Gratification Culture: Social media and on-demand entertainment reduce patience for delayed gratification.

Marketing Sophistication: Children face advertising designed by psychologists to trigger impulse purchases.

Peer Pressure Amplification: Social media makes lifestyle comparison constant and global rather than limited to immediate peer groups.

Strategies for Digital Age Financial Education

Make Money Tangible

- Use cash for younger children to maintain physical connection to money
- Show bank balances and investment account changes regularly
- Create visual representations of savings goals and progress

Build Patience Muscles

- Implement waiting periods for non-essential purchases

- Create savings challenges with specific goals and timelines
- Celebrate delayed gratification successes

Develop Marketing Immunity

- Discuss advertising techniques and psychological manipulation
- Practice evaluating purchases based on value rather than emotion
- Create "cooling off" periods for impulse purchase desires

Reframe Social Comparison

- Focus on values and goals rather than possessions
- Teach that everyone's financial situation is different and private
- Emphasize personal progress over relative comparison

THE INHERITANCE CONVERSATION: WHEN & HOW DO I DISCUSS FAMILY WEALTH?

The question wealthy parents face: when do you tell your children about their potential inheritance?

Before Age 16…Too Early!

- You'll risk creating entitlement and reducing motivation to develop their own capabilities

After Age 25...Too Late!

- You can shock them with responsibilities they're unprepared to handle

From the Ages of 16 to 22...Just right!

- Old enough to understand responsibility, young enough to influence their development

THE GRADUAL DISCLOSURE APPROACH

Age 16: «Our family has been successful financially, which creates opportunities and responsibilities.»

Age 18: «Here's approximately what our family is worth and how it's structured.»

Age 20: «Here's what you might inherit someday and what we expect from you as a result.»

Age 22: «Here's how you can begin participating in family financial decisions.»

Important Tips

1. **Setting Inheritance Expectations:** Successful wealth transfer requires clear expectations about inheritance.

2. **Education Requirements:** Access to family wealth requires completing education and demonstrating financial competence.
3. **Value Alignment:** «Your actions should reflect our family values of hard work, integrity, and service to others.»

4. **Contribution Expectation:** «You're expected to contribute meaningfully to society through work, service, or value creation.»
5. **Stewardship Responsibility:** «This wealth isn't just yours—you're a steward for future generations.»

THE FAMILY WEALTH CONSTITUTION

Some families formalize their values and expectations in a written Family Wealth Constitution, a document that outlines the following,

1. Family mission and values
2. Expectations for family members
3. Guidelines for wealth access and use
4. Conflict resolution processes
5. Charitable giving commitments

This document serves as a reference point for difficult decisions and helps maintain family unity across generations.

COMMON PITFALLS AND HOW TO AVOID THEM

Pitfall #1, Overindulgence: Giving children everything they want without teaching them to work for it

Solution: Connect purchases to effort and create opportunities for earning

Pitfall #2, Financial Secrecy: Keeping all financial information private until children are adults

Solution: Age-appropriate transparency that builds understanding gradually

Pitfall #3, Perfectionism: Expecting children to never make financial mistakes

Solution: Create safe environments for making and learning from small mistakes

Pitfall #4, Comparison Pressure: Constantly comparing your children's financial behavior to others

Solution: Focus on personal growth and progress rather than relative performance

YOUR FAMILY FINANCIAL EDUCATION ACTION PLAN

Ages 3-7

- Implement three-jar system for money allocation
- Create work-for-money opportunities
- Include children in age-appropriate spending decisions
- Begin charity involvement

Ages 8-12

- Open savings account and discuss interest regularly
- Encourage entrepreneurial projects
- Teach comparison shopping and value assessment
- Introduce basic investing concepts through games

Ages 13-17

- Require part-time work experience

- Provide real budget management responsibility
- Open custodial investment account
- Include in family financial discussions as observer

Ages 18-25

- Transition to financial independence gradually
- Provide mentorship but allow real consequences
- Include in family investment decisions
- Begin inheritance discussions

UNDERSTANDING THE COMPOUND EFFECT OF FINANCIAL EDUCATION

The investment you make in your children's financial education compounds over their lifetime, just like money in the market. A child who understands delayed gratification at age seven becomes an adult who know how to build wealth through systematic investing. A teenager who learns how to create value through work becomes an entrepreneur who creates generational wealth.

Brooke is now sixteen. She has a part-time job, manages her own budget, and contributes to family investment discussions. More importantly, she sees money as a tool for creating opportunities and helping others, instead of a source of stress or entitlement.

When she inevitably inherits wealth someday, she will be prepared to be a good steward. Not because I told her what to do, but because she learned how to think about money through years of age-appropriate experience and education.

That conversation at Giants Stadium started a process that will serve her for the rest of her life. The question "Are we rich?" led to an understanding that wealth is about choices, responsibility, and impact rather than just accumulation.

Your children are watching how you think about money, talk about money, and use money. They're forming beliefs and habits that will guide their financial decisions for decades. The question is not whether you should educate your children about money, it is whether you will do it intentionally or leave it to chance.

The choice you make today determines whether your wealth becomes a blessing or a burden for the people you love most.

CHAPTER 9

Building Generational Wealth Systems

"Systems turn generational wealth into a dynasty —chaos turns it to dust."

THE PHONE CALL THAT REVEALED EVERYTHING

At 7:23 AM on a Saturday morning, my phone rang with a number I didn't recognize. The voice on the other end was shaking with barely contained rage.

"Mr. Ruiz? This is Jennifer Martinez. My father just died, and I'm calling every financial advisor in his contact list because I can't figure out what the hell he left us."

Jennifer's father, Carlos, had been a client for eight years. He had built a successful landscaping business from a single pickup truck into a million-dollar operation. He owned rental properties, had substantial investment accounts, and had always talked about leaving his children "set for life."

But as Jennifer's story unfolded over the next hour, I realized Carlos had made the classic mistake that destroys generational wealth: he had built assets without building systems.

"I found fourteen different bank accounts," Jennifer continued, her voice cracking with frustration. "Investment accounts at five different companies. Properties I didn't even know existed. A business partnership agreement I can't understand. And my brother and sister are already fighting about who gets what."

Carlos had accumulated wealth, but he had not architected a wealth system. The difference would cost his family thousands of dollars and practically destroy their relationships.

THE GENERATIONAL WEALTH PARADOX

90% of wealthy families lose their wealth by the third generation is a brutal truth about generational wealth. This is not because of market crashes, economic downturns, or bad luck. It is because they confuse having money with having wealth systems.

Money is temporary. Systems are permanent.

Carlos had money. The Rothschild family has systems. Guess which approach creates wealth that lasts centuries?

The Four Pillars of Generational Wealth Systems

After analyzing hundreds of successful multi-generational families, I have identified four essential pillars that separate families who preserve wealth from those who lose it,

Pillar 1, Wealth Architecture: Structured systems for growing, protecting, and transferring assets across generations

Pillar 2, Family Governance: Formal processes for decision-making, conflict resolution, and family unity

Pillar 3, Next-Generation Development: Systematic preparation of heirs to receive, manage, and multiply inherited wealth

Pillar 4, Legacy Preservation: Values, stories, and traditions that maintain family identity and purpose across generations

Most families focus exclusively on Pillar 1, while completely ignoring Pillars 2, 3, and 4. This imbalance explains why wealth rarely survives generational transfer.

PILLAR 1: WEALTH ARCHITECTURE

BUILDING THE FOUNDATION

Wealth architecture goes beyond simple asset accumulation. It involves creating integrated systems that optimize for tax efficiency, risk management, growth potential, and transfer flexibility.

THE FAMILY BALANCE SHEET APPROACH

Instead of managing individual accounts and investments, generational wealth families think in terms of integrated balance sheets that serve multiple purposes across multiple generations.

Assets Layer

- Operating businesses and their growth potential
- Investment portfolios optimized for long-term compound growth
- Real estate holdings for income and inflation protection

- Alternative investments for diversification and yield enhancement

Structure Layer

- Trust structures for tax optimization and asset protection
- Business entities for operational efficiency and liability management
- Insurance strategies for risk transfer and wealth replacement
- Geographic diversification for political and economic risk management

Control Layer

- Governance documents that specify decision-making authority
- Investment policies that maintain discipline across market cycles
- Succession plans that ensure smooth leadership transitions
- Family employment policies that balance opportunity with merit

Case Study: The Johnson Family Wealth Architecture

The Johnson family has built wealth through a chain of hardware stores across the Midwest. Instead of simply accumulating individual wealth, they created the following integrated system:

Operating Company: Johnson Hardware Holdings LLC owns all store locations and operations

Investment Company: Johnson Family Investments manages liquid investments and new opportunities

Real Estate Holdings: Johnson Properties owns all real estate, leasing to operating company for tax advantages

Family Foundation: Johnson Foundation handles charitable giving and family values development

Trust Structure: Generation-skipping trusts minimize estate taxes across multiple generations

Family Council: Formal governance body making major strategic decisions

This architecture allows the family to:

- Optimize tax efficiency across all entities
- Protect assets from individual liability exposure
- Create multiple income streams for family members
- Maintain control while distributing ownership
- Plan for smooth generational transitions

The Compound Growth Optimization System

Generational wealth systems are designed to compound not just money, but capability, wisdom, and impact across generations.

Financial Compounding: Assets structured to grow efficiently over decades

Knowledge Compounding: Each generation builds on previous knowledge and experience

Network Compounding: Family relationships and business connections expand exponentially

Impact Compounding: Family influence and contribution to society multiply over time

PILLAR 2: FAMILY GOVERNANCE, THE OPERATING SYSTEM

Family governance is the operating system that allows wealthy families to make decisions, resolve conflicts, and maintain unity across generations. Without formal governance, families drift into chaos as they grow larger and more complex.

THE FAMILY CONSTITUTION

A "family constitution" is a written document that serves as the family's "operating manual." It outlines,

Family Mission and Values: Why the family exists and what principles guide their decisions

Membership Criteria: Who is considered part of the family for governance purposes

Decision-Making Processes: How major decisions are made and who has authority

Conflict Resolution Procedures: How disagreements are addressed constructively

Employment Policies: Guidelines for family members working in family businesses

Wealth Access Guidelines: Criteria for accessing family financial resources

Communication Standards: How information is shared and meetings are conducted

THE MARTINEZ FAMILY CONSTITUTION EXAMPLE

After Carlos' chaotic estate situation, his children and I created the following family constitution to prevent future problems:

Mission Statement: «The Martinez family exists to honor our father's entrepreneurial spirit by building businesses that create value for our community, while providing opportunities for family members to contribute their talents."

Core Values:

- Entrepreneurship and value creation
- Education and personal development
- Community service and social responsibility
- Family unity and mutual support

Decision-Making Structure:

- Family Council, made up of all adult family members, for major strategic decisions
- Investment Committee made up of three elected members) for financial management

- Next-Gen Board, made up of family members under 35, for innovation and development

Employment Policy: Family members can work in family businesses only after gaining outside experience and demonstrating competence

Wealth Access Guidelines: Family funds available for education, business ventures, and emergencies with approval process

The Family Council: Democracy with Structure

The Family Council serves as the family's board of directors and make major decisions about wealth management, business strategy, and family policies.

TYPICAL FAMILY COUNCIL STRUCTURE:

Membership: All adult family members (typically 18+)

Leadership: Rotating chairperson elected for 2–3-year terms

Meeting Frequency: Quarterly for routine business, annually for strategic planning

Decision Authority:

- Major investment decisions above specified thresholds
- Changes to family constitution or governance policies
- Approval of family member business proposals
- Charitable giving strategy and major donations

- Conflict resolution for disputes between family members

Voting Structure: Varies by family, but typically one vote per person regardless of wealth ownership

Family Communication Systems

Successful multi-generational families create formal communication systems to keep everyone informed and engaged. Use these tools to do the same,

Quarterly Family Newsletter: Updates on business performance, family activities, and upcoming decisions

Annual Family Meeting: In-person gathering for strategic planning, education, and relationship building

Family Intranet: Private website with financial reports, governance documents, and family history

Regular Family Calls: Monthly conference calls for routine updates and coordination

Educational Programs: Seminars, workshops, and external education opportunities

PILLAR 3: NEXT-GENERATION DEVELOPMENT - PREPARING FUTURE STEWARDS

The most critical element of generational wealth preservation is preparing the next generation to receive, manage, and multiply their inheritance.

THE DEVELOPMENT PIPELINE

Successful families create formal development programs that build capability and character across multiple generations:

Ages 8-15: Foundation Building

- Financial literacy education appropriate for age
- Exposure to family businesses and investments
- Community service and charitable involvement
- Character development through challenges and responsibility

Ages 16-22: Skill Development

- External work experience to build competence
- Formal education with family financial support
- Mentorship relationships with successful non-family members
- Increasing involvement in family governance activities

Ages 23-30: Capability Demonstration

- Independent career success before family business involvement
- Leadership roles in family charitable activities
- Investment committee participation and learning
- Formal evaluation of readiness for increased responsibility

Ages 30+: Leadership Transition

- Eligible for senior leadership roles in family enterprises
- Full participation in family governance decisions
- Mentorship responsibility for younger family members
- Legacy planning and wealth transfer preparation

The Performance-Based Development Model

Instead of automatic inheritance based on bloodline, leading families implement performance-based development that rewards contribution and competence:

Education Milestones: Completion of relevant education with family financial support

Experience Requirements: Demonstrated success in non-family employment or entrepreneurship

Values Alignment: Behavior consistent with family values and constitution

Contribution Metrics: Meaningful participation in family governance and activities

Leadership Demonstration: Proven ability to lead projects and work with others effectively

The Mentorship System

Successful families create formal mentorship relationships that accelerate development:

Internal Mentors: Senior family members guide junior members in family-specific knowledge

External Mentors: Successful non-family professionals provide outside perspective and guidance

Peer Mentors: Family members close in age support each other's development

Professional Mentors: Industry experts provide specialized knowledge and skills

Reverse Mentors: Younger family members teach technology and new thinking to senior members

CASE STUDY: THE CHEN FAMILY DEVELOPMENT PROGRAM

The Chen family created a comprehensive development program for their three children:

Foundation Phase (Ages 12-18):

- Summer jobs in different industries that are not within family businesses
- Financial literacy curriculum including investing and entrepreneurship
- Community service requirement: 100 hours annually
- Family business observation without decision-making authority

Development Phase (Ages 18-25):

- College education with family support contingent on maintaining standards
- Study abroad semester to build global perspective
- Two-year external work requirement before family business eligibility
- Family foundation board participation with limited voting rights

Transition Phase (Ages 25-35):

- Eligible for family business positions based on performance and need
- Full family council participation and voting rights
- Investment committee involvement with increasing responsibility
- Mentorship roles for younger family members and community youth

Leadership Phase (Ages 35+):

- Eligible for senior leadership positions in family enterprises
- Full authority in areas of demonstrated competence
- Responsibility for developing next generation
- Legacy planning and wealth transfer authority

Results: All three Chen children developed successful independent careers before joining family businesses. They work together effectively because they earned their positions through merit rather than inheritance.

Pillar 4: Legacy Preservation to Ensure Values and Identity

The final pillar involves preserving the intangible elements that give wealth meaning like family values, stories, traditions, and identity.

THE FAMILY STORY: WHY NARRATIVE MATTERS

Every family has an origin story that explains how wealth was created and why it matters. These stories become the foundation of family identity and values:

Origin Story Elements

- How the founding generation created wealth
- What challenges they overcame
- What values guided their decisions
- What they hoped to achieve for their families
- What lessons they learned from failures and successes

Story Preservation Methods

- Recorded interviews with founding generation
- Written family history documents
- Photo and document archives

- Annual storytelling traditions
- Integration into family education programs

VALUES-BASED DECISION MAKING

Successful multi-generational families make decisions based on values rather than just financial optimization:

Value-Based Investment Policies: Investment strategies that reflect family values like ESG investing or avoiding certain industries.

Philanthropic Legacy: Charitable giving that reflects family passions and values.

Business Ethics Standards: Operating businesses according to family principles.

Employment Practices: Treating employees and communities according to family values.

Community Involvement: Using wealth and influence to benefit community according to family mission.

The Tradition Creation Process

Families can intentionally create traditions that reinforce values and maintain unity:

Annual Family Retreats: Extended time together focused on relationships and planning.

Coming-of-Age Ceremonies: Formal recognition when family members reach development milestones.

Storytelling Dinners: Regular gatherings where family history and values are shared.

Service Projects: Shared work on charitable or community improvement activities.

Business Learning Experiences: Visits to family enterprises and investment properties.

Integration Challenge: Making the System Work

The four pillars must work together seamlessly to create effective generational wealth systems:

Architecture without Governance: Creates wealthy individuals but not wealthy families

Governance without Development: Maintains control but doesn't prepare successors

Development without Legacy: Builds capable people but loses family identity

Legacy without Architecture: Preserves values but loses financial foundation

THE IMPLEMENTATION TIMELINE

Building generational wealth systems takes years, but the process can begin immediately by following this timeline,

Year 1: Foundation

- Create basic governance documents (family constitution)

- Establish family council and communication systems
- Begin next-generation development programs
- Document family story and values

Years 2-3: Development

- Implement formal mentorship and education programs
- Create investment policies and financial architecture
- Establish charitable giving strategies
- Build family traditions and communication systems

Years 4-5: Optimization

- Refine governance systems based on experience
- Advance next-generation development and responsibility
- Optimize tax and legal structures
- Evaluate and improve family communication effectiveness

Years 6+: Evolution

- Transition leadership to next generation gradually
- Adapt systems to changing family size and complexity
- Maintain and evolve family traditions and values
- Prepare for multi-generational wealth transfer

THE JOHNSON FAMILY: TEN YEARS LATER

Remember the Johnson family hardware stores? Ten years after implementing their generational wealth system, these were the following results in each category,

Business: Grown from 12 stores to 31 stores across four states.

Family: Three generations working together effectively in various roles.

Governance: Family council makes major decisions by consensus with minimal conflict.

Development: Six family members in leadership development pipeline.

Legacy: Family foundation has donated over $2 million to community education.

Conflict: Two major disagreements resolved through family governance process without litigation.

THE COST OF NOT BUILDING SYSTEMS

Remember Carlos Martinez from the opening story? The final accounting of his estate settlement:

Legal Fees: $180,000 for probate and family conflict resolution

Tax Inefficiency: $95,000 in unnecessary estate and income taxes

Asset Liquidation: $240,000 lost from forced sale of business at unfavorable terms

Family Relationships: Two siblings still not speaking eighteen months later

Lost Opportunity: Estimated $500,000 in growth potential lost during transition chaos

> ***Total Cost of No System: Over $1 million in financial losses plus immeasurable family pain.***

To avoid repeating the same mistakes, follow this action plan,

YOUR GENERATIONAL WEALTH SYSTEM ACTION PLAN

Month 1-3: Assessment and Planning

- Evaluate current wealth structure and identify system gaps
- Begin family conversations about values and governance
- Research legal and tax optimization opportunities
- Start documenting family story and values

Month 4-6: Foundation Building

- Create family constitution draft with professional help
- Establish basic governance structure, i.e. family council
- Implement next-generation development assessment
- Begin family communication systems

Month 7-12: Implementation

- Finalize legal structures and tax optimization strategies
- Launch formal governance and communication systems

- Begin next-generation mentorship and development programs
- Establish charitable giving and family foundation plans

Year 2+: Evolution and Optimization

- Refine systems based on family experience and feedback
- Expand next-generation development and responsibility
- Build family traditions and legacy preservation activities
- Plan for leadership transition and succession

THE CHOICE THAT DEFINES GENERATIONS

Jennifer Martinez learned the hard way that creating wealth without systems is just temporary accumulation. After spending two years untangling her father's financial chaos, she committed to building the systems he never created.

"I won't let my children go through what we went through," she told me recently. "Dad worked too hard building wealth for us to let it disappear in one generation."

Today, the Martinez family has a constitution, governance system, and development programs for the next generation. Additionally, they now have a clear mission that honors their father's entrepreneurial legacy while also preparing for their own.

The Johnson family has built wealth that will last centuries because they built systems that can evolve and adapt across generations.

The Chen family raised children who are prepared to be good stewards of wealth because they were developed systematically rather than randomly.

The choice every wealth builder faces: Will you create assets that disappear in one generation, or will you build systems that create wealth for centuries?

The difference between the two determines whether your hard work becomes a temporary blessing or a permanent legacy.

Your family's wealth system is waiting to be built. The only question is: will you build it intentionally, or will you leave it to chance?

CHAPTER 10

The 2:47 AM Call That Changes Everything

"The 2:47 AM call isn't just a wake-up —it's your chance to rewrite your family's future."

WHEN DEATH REVEALS WHAT LIFE CONCEALED

This call came in at 2:47 AM on a Tuesday morning. I knew before I answered that someone's world had just irreversibly changed.

"Mijo," my father muttered. His voice was different—quieter, more deliberate than I had ever heard it. "We need to talk. There are things I need to show you."

Six months earlier, he had been invincible. He still had the magnetic force I remembered from my childhood. He could still negotiate a real estate deal over café con leche and still make it to Brooke's lacrosse game by sunset.

Cancer has a way of stripping everything down to what truly matters. What mattered to my father in those final months was not the buildings he had accumulated or the businesses he had built, but the blueprint he was about to hand down.

I drove through empty Newark streets at 3 AM as my mind raced faster than my Honda Accord. What could be so urgent that it could not wait until morning? What "things" needed to be shown in the middle of the night?

When I arrived at his house, every light was on. He was sitting at the kitchen table—the same one where my mother had counted crumpled bills decades earlier—surrounded by documents, folders, and scattered pieces of a financial empire I never knew existed.

"Sit down," he said, gesturing to the chair across from him. "What I'm about to show you will either make our family's fortune last for generations, or it will all disappear within ten years of my death."

That's when I learned the most important financial lesson of my life: **Wealth is not what you leave behind, it is what you leave inside people.**

THE THREE STACKS THAT DEFINE EVERYTHING

On the table before us were three distinct stacks of papers.

Stack One: "The Empire"

- Deeds to fourteen properties I did not know he owned
- Business partnership agreements for companies I had never heard of
- Bank statements showing balances that made my head spin

- Investment accounts scattered across six different firms

Stack Two: "The Protection"

- Life insurance policies worth more than most people will earn in a lifetime
- Trust documents with my name as successor trustee
- Powers of attorney that gave me control over his entire financial world
- A will that had been updated more recently than I had updated my iPhone

Stack Three: "The Wisdom"

- Handwritten letters to each of his grandchildren
- A detailed explanation of every financial decision he had ever made
- Instructions for how to preserve and grow what he had built
- A document he called "The Family Operating System"

"The first stack," he said, his calloused finger tapping the property deeds, "is what everyone sees. The money. The buildings. The 'stuff' that makes people think you're successful."

He moved to the second stack. "This is what protects the first stack from taxes, lawsuits, and stupidity that destroys most family wealth within one generation."

Then his hand rested on the third stack, and his voice dropped to almost a whisper. "But this—this is what determines whether your children's children will thank us or curse us. Whether they'll be empowered by what we built or destroyed by it."

I stared at the three stacks, suddenly understanding why my father had called me at 2:47 AM. This was not just about money. This was about the architecture of legacy, which illustrated the difference between leaving wealth and leaving wisdom.

THE $2.3 MILLION MISTAKE THAT HAUNTED HIM

"Let me tell you about David Chen," my father said, pulling out a newspaper clipping from 2019. "Successful businessman. Built a tech consulting company from nothing. Reminded me of myself when I was younger."

David had died suddenly at fifty-eight from a heart attack in his office on a Saturday morning while reviewing quarterly reports. He had accumulated $2.3 million across various accounts, owned three properties, and had a business worth another $800,000.

"His family should have been set for life," my father continued, his voice growing harder.

"Instead, they lost over a million dollars because David never did what I'm doing with you right now."

The financial devastation was swift and merciless:

- **Estate taxes consumed $460,000** because David had not used his lifetime exemption
- **Probate costs ate another $115,000** because assets weren't properly titled

- **Family fighting cost $180,000 in legal fees** because his intentions weren't clear
- **Business partnership disputes consumed $320,000** when forced liquidation occurred

"David's family received $1.22 million of his $2.3 million estate," my father said, sliding the newspaper clipping across the table.

"Almost half of his life's work disappeared into the machinery of an inefficient system."

The tragedy? All of it could have been prevented with proper planning that would have cost less than $15,000.

"That," my father said, pointing at the clipping, "is why you're here at 3 AM instead of sleeping in your warm bed."

THE DOCUMENTS THAT SPEAK WHEN YOU CANNOT

My father opened the protection stack and spread out a collection of legal documents that looked like they could fill a small library.

"Most people think estate planning is about death," he said. "It's not. It's about control. It's about making sure your wishes are followed when you can't speak to them yourself."

THE LAST WILL AND TESTAMENT: YOUR FINAL VOICE

"This," he said, holding up a thick document bound in blue legal backing, "is my voice when I no longer have one."

His will wasn't just a list of who gets what. It was a carefully orchestrated plan for:

- **Distribution of assets** that are not covered by other documents
- **Guardianship instructions** for minor grandchildren if something happened to their parents
- **Executor powers** that would allow seamless management during transition
- **Charitable bequests** that reflected our family's values
- **Personal property distribution** that would prevent fights over sentimental items

"But here's what most people don't understand," he continued. "A will only controls assets that don't have other instructions already attached to them."

THE TRUST: YOUR WEALTH'S OPERATING SYSTEM

Next came a document that looked like it had been drafted by constitutional lawyers: *"The Ruiz Family Revocable Living Trust."*

"Think of this like creating a corporation for our family wealth," he explained. "I remain in complete control while I'm alive and competent. But if I become incapacitated or die, this trust provides structure for management and distribution."

The benefits were staggering:

- **Probate avoidance**: Assets would transfer immediately to beneficiaries, not in 18 months after court approval
- **Privacy protection**: Trust terms would remain confidential, unlike wills which become public record

- **Incapacity planning**: If he could not make decisions, I could step in seamlessly
- **Tax optimization**: Structured to minimize estate and generation-skipping taxes
- **Professional management**: Provisions for hiring investment managers if needed

"Your mother and I lived through probate when my father died," he said, his voice growing distant. "Eighteen months of lawyers, court dates, and family arguments over a $150,000 estate. I swore my children would never go through that."

POWERS OF ATTORNEY: YOUR EMERGENCY DEPUTIES

Two more documents emerged from the stack. These papers that looked deceptively simple but carried enormous power.

"Financial Power of Attorney," he said, sliding the first document toward me. "If I'm in a coma tomorrow, you can access every account, pay every bill, and make every financial decision as if you were me."

The second document was even more sobering: "Healthcare Power of Attorney".

"This authorizes you to make medical decisions if I can't. Life support. Treatment options. End-of-life care. The doctors will look to you, not to some court-appointed guardian."

He paused, letting the weight of that responsibility settle between us.

"Without these documents, your family would need to hire lawyers, file for conservatorship, wait months for court approval, and pay ongoing supervision fees just to access my bank account to pay for my medical care."

THE BENEFICIARY DESIGNATION TRAP

From a manila folder, my father pulled out forms that looked like they'd been updated more recently than his will.

"Every retirement account, life insurance policy, and bank account has beneficiary designations," he said. "These forms override everything else—your will, your trust, your family's wishes."

He showed me a case study that had haunted him for years: Mark Rodriguez, a friend who had divorced and remarried but forgot to change the beneficiary on his $500,000 401(k) account.

"When Mark died, his current wife got nothing from his largest asset," my father said. "His ex-wife, who he hadn't spoken to in fifteen years, received half a million dollars because a simple form wasn't updated."

Every account my father owned had been reviewed and updated within the past year:

- **Primary and contingent beneficiaries** on every account
- **Percentage allocations** instead of dollar amounts (accounts grow over time)
- **Trust naming** for minor beneficiaries who couldn't handle large inheritances
- **Per stirpes designations** ensuring grandchildren would inherit if their parents predeceased him

"I spend thirty minutes twice a year reviewing these," he said. "Thirty minutes that could save my family millions and years of heartache."

THE TAX MONSTER THAT DEVOURS LEGACIES

"Now comes the part that will make you angry," my father said, opening a thick folder labeled "Tax Planning."

Federal estate tax could consume 40% of wealth above $13.61 million per person in 2024. But the exemption was scheduled to drop to approximately $7 million in 2026 unless Congress acted.

"I'm not worth thirteen million," I said, confused about why this mattered.

"You're not thinking like a wealth builder," he replied. "You're twenty-eight years old. If you follow what I'm teaching you, you could easily accumulate that much by retirement. But more importantly, twelve states have their own estate taxes with much lower thresholds."

He showed me the numbers:

- **Oregon**: $1 million exemption
- **Massachusetts**: $2 million exemption
- **Rhode Island**: $1.733 million exemption

"Families in these states face estate tax liability at wealth levels that good planning and investing can easily achieve," he explained.

THE SECURE ACT BOMB

But the real shock came when he explained what Congress had done to inherited retirement accounts.

"The SECURE Act of 2019 created a tax time bomb for families like ours," he said, his voice carrying the weight of someone who'd seen the damage firsthand.

Before 2020, beneficiaries could "stretch" inherited IRA withdrawals over their lifetime. A 30-year-old inheriting $500,000 could withdraw about $15,000 annually for decades, paying taxes at normal rates.

"Now," he continued, "most beneficiaries must empty inherited accounts within ten years. That same $500,000 becomes $50,000 in forced annual withdrawals, potentially pushing beneficiaries into much higher tax brackets."

He showed me a calculation that made my stomach drop: a beneficiary who inherited a $500,000 IRA under the new rules could pay $200,000 more in taxes over ten years compared to the old system.

"This is why I've been converting traditional IRAs to Roth IRAs," he explained. "I pay the taxes now while I'm in control, so you and Brooke inherit tax-free growth instead of tax-deferred problems."

THE STORY THAT STARTED IT ALL

As dawn broke through the kitchen windows, my father's voice grew softer, more reflective.

"You want to know why I called you at 2:47 AM? Why this couldn't wait until morning?"

He reached into the wisdom stack and pulled out a handwritten letter addressed to me.

"Because I learned something from David Chen's death that changed everything. His family told me that three weeks before he died, David had said he needed to 'get his affairs in order.' He had scheduled a meeting with an estate planning attorney for the Monday after he died."

The silence hung heavy between us.

"David thought he had time," my father continued. "He thought planning could wait until he was ready, until he had more clarity, until the perfect moment presented itself."

He slid the letter across the table.

"I don't know how much time I have left, mijo. The doctors give me estimates, but God keeps His own schedule. What I know is this: every day I delay preparing you for this responsibility is a day I steal from our family's future."

THE LETTER THAT CHANGED MY LIFE

My hands shook as I opened the envelope. Inside was my father's distinctive handwriting—the same careful script he had used to track tire shop earnings decades earlier.

> *"Mijo,*
>
> *If you're reading this, then I've moved on to whatever comes next. But before I go, I want you to know what you meant to my life, and what I hope you'll do with the foundation we built together.*
>
> *The money is just a tool. The buildings are just assets. The real inheritance is the understanding that wealth without wisdom becomes a curse, not a blessing.*
>
> *I didn't have anyone to teach me about trusts and estate taxes and family governance. I learned by making mistakes that cost us opportunities and peace of mind. You don't have to make those same mistakes.*
>
> *But more than that, I want you to understand why preserving this wealth matters. It's not about the money itself—it's about the choices money creates. For your daughter Brooke. For grandchildren I may never meet. For the impact our family can have on the world.*

Use what we built wisely. Teach Brooke what I'm teaching you. And when the time comes, pass on not just the wealth, but the responsibility that comes with it.

This is how families create legacies that last for centuries instead of disappearing in one generation.

Todo para ustedes—everything for all of you.

Con amor y orgullo, Papa"

I could not finish reading it without my tears blurring every words.

THE THREE HECTORS AND THE WEIGHT OF LEGACY

"You know why I named all three of my sons Hector?" my father asked as I composed myself.

I'd always assumed it was tradition, or maybe ego, or possibly a lack of imagination.

"Because I wanted you to understand that you're not just individuals building your own lives. You're links in a chain that started before you were born and will continue long after you're gone."

He gestured to the documents spread across the table.

"Everything I'm showing you tonight—the planning, the protection, the preparation—it's not just about preserving what I built. It's about creating a platform that lets the next generation build something even greater."

THE 70% FAILURE RATE

"Here's a statistic that should terrify every parent building wealth," my father said, pulling out a research report from the Family Business Institute.

"70% of wealthy families lose their wealth by the second generation. 90% lose it by the third generation."

The numbers hit like a physical blow. All that work, all that sacrifice, all those years of building—gone within decades.

"This isn't about market crashes or economic downturns," he continued. "It's about families who accumulate assets without developing systems. They leave money but not meaning. Wealth but not wisdom."

He showed me the three primary causes of wealth destruction:

1. **Unprepared heirs** who inherit money without inheriting the skills to manage it.

2. **Family conflicts** that turn siblings into adversaries and tear families apart.

3. **Lack of purpose** that makes wealth feel like a burden instead of a blessing.

"That," he said, pointing at the wisdom stack, "is why this conversation is happening. Because I refuse to let our family become a statistic."

THE FAMILY OPERATING SYSTEM

The final document my father shared was unlike anything I'd seen—a handwritten manual he called "The Family Operating System."

It wasn't a legal document. It wasn't a financial plan. It was a blueprint for how our family would make decisions, resolve conflicts, and maintain unity across generations.

Family Mission Statement: *"The Ruiz family exists to honor our immigrant heritage by building businesses that create value for* *our community while providing opportunities for family members to contribute their talents and develop their character."*

Core Values

- Entrepreneurship and value creation
- Education and personal development
- Community service and social responsibility
- Family unity and mutual support
- Financial responsibility and stewardship

Decision-Making Framework

- Major financial decisions require consultation with family council
- Business opportunities evaluated based on family mission and values
- Charitable giving coordinated to maximize impact and teach stewardship
- Conflict resolution through structured family meetings, not lawyers

Employment Guidelines

- Family members must gain outside experience before joining family businesses
- Positions earned through competence, not birthright

- Performance held to higher standards, not lower ones
- Mentorship and development provided, but excellence required

Wealth Access Principles

- Education funding available for legitimate learning opportunities
- Business capital available for viable ventures with proper planning
- Emergency support available with repayment expectations
- Lifestyle funding earned through contribution and achievement

I'm not trying to make decisions for people who aren't born yet," my father said. "I'm creating guardrails that help everyone stay on track when life gets complicated."

THE CONVERSATION THAT WILL DEFINE GENERATIONS

As we finished organizing the documents and the morning sun filled the kitchen with light, my father asked me a question that would haunt me for years,

"What do you want Brooke to remember about money and family and responsibility?"

I thought about my eleven-year-old daughter, who still believed that wealth and success were simple and straightforward.

"I want her to understand that money is a tool, not a goal," I said slowly. "I want her to feel empowered by what we've built, not burdened by it. I want her to know that with privilege comes responsibility."

"Then you need to start teaching her now," my father said. "Not when she's twenty-five and inherits a trust fund. Not when she's eighteen and leaves for college. Now, while her beliefs about money and family and responsibility are still forming."

THE LEGACY LAB: TEACHING BROOKE ABOUT WEALTH

That conversation launched what I now call our family's "Legacy Lab"—a systematic approach to preparing the next generation for wealth stewardship.

Age 11-15

Foundation Building: We started with basic concepts wrapped in age-appropriate experiences:

Family Investment Committee: Brooke joined our quarterly portfolio reviews as an observer, learning that investing was methodical, not magical.

Charity Board Participation: She helped choose recipients for our annual giving, learning that wealth carries the responsibility to help others.

Business Exposure: Summer days at construction sites and property visits, understanding that money comes from creating value for others.

Financial Decision Involvement: When we bought our current house, Brooke participated in the decision-making process, learning about mortgages, property taxes, and long-term planning.

THE GREAT ALLOWANCE NEGOTIATION

When my client Sarah announced that her 9-year-old son Marcus had just presented her with a formal PowerPoint presentation titled "Why My Allowance Should Be Performance-Based", I knew we'd entered uncharted territory in financial education.

Marcus had apparently spent two weeks researching how professional athletes get paid and concluded that flat-rate allowances were "economically inefficient" and proposed a revolutionary new system: base pay plus bonuses for exceptional performance.

His slide deck included:

- Market research (what his friends earned)
- Performance metrics (grades, chores completed, "attitude scores")
- Bonus structure (extra credit for going above and beyond)
- A pie chart showing optimal fund allocation

"He actually cited supply and demand theory," Sarah told me, equal parts impressed and terrified. "My fourth grader is out-negotiating me using economics principles."

THE ENTREPRENEUR IN TRAINING

Rather than shutting down Marcus' initiative, Sarah decided to lean into it. They spent a Saturday morning hammering out what became known as "The Marcus Employment Contract":

Base Salary: $8 weekly for essential family contributions (keeping his room organized, setting the dinner table, basic courtesy to siblings)

Performance Bonuses

- $2 for all A's on weekly progress reports
- $1 for completing homework without reminders
- $3 for identifying and solving a household problem nobody asked him to solve

Penalty System: Sarah would apply late fees for missed chores and quality deductions for half-hearted work.

The Twist: Marcus had to track his own performance and calculate his weekly earnings, then present them to Sarah for approval.

THE UNEXPECTED LESSONS

Within a month, Marcus had learned lessons no traditional allowance could teach:

Week 1: He earned $6 total because he'd overestimated his performance and had to revise his calculations downward when Sarah reviewed his work quality.

Week 2: He identified that the family's recycling system was chaotic and reorganized the entire garage setup, earning his first $3 problem-solving bonus.

Week 3: Marcus lobbied for a mid-contract negotiation, arguing that inflation should trigger cost-of-living adjustments to his base salary. Sarah agreed to review annually.

Week 4: He started helping his younger sister with her homework—not for bonus money, but because he realized that family success made everyone's life easier.

THE BUSINESS EXPANSION

By month three, Marcus had evolved from employee to entrepreneur. He started a neighborhood pet-sitting service, created a referral network with friends for yard work, and began saving money in what he called his "business development fund."

"I'm not paying him to be a good kid anymore," Sarah told me six months later. "He's become a good kid because he understands how value creation works. The money just follows naturally."

Marcus learned that sustainable income comes from solving problems for other people, that quality work commands premium prices, and that reputation is the most valuable business asset.

Most importantly, he discovered that the best financial education happens when kids stop seeing money as something adults give them and start seeing it as something they can earn through contribution.

"Dad always said I was too young to understand business," Marcus told Sarah recently. "But I think adults just explain it wrong. It's not complicated—you just have to make people's lives better and they'll pay you for it."

Sometimes the best financial wisdom comes from nine-year-olds with PowerPoint skills.

THE INHERITANCE CONVERSATION

When Brooke turned thirteen, I finally had the conversation with her that my father had taught me to have.

"Brooke, our family has been successful financially, which creates both opportunities and responsibilities for you."

I explained in age-appropriate terms that she would likely inherit substantial wealth someday. But I also explained what I expected from her,

"This wealth isn't just yours to spend however you want," I said. "You're going to be a steward of something that took generations to build. That means you need to prepare yourself to be worthy of that responsibility."

Education Requirements: Excellence in school, understanding of financial principles, demonstrated maturity in decision-making.

Value Alignment: Behavior that reflects our family values of hard work, integrity, and service to others.

Contribution Expectation: Using her advantages to create value for others, not just to consume resources.

Stewardship Responsibility: Understanding that she's managing wealth for future generations, not just for herself.

"I'm not trying to control your life," I explained. "I'm trying to prepare you for the life that's coming, whether you choose it or not."

WHEN YOUR TEENAGER STARTS THINKING LIKE AN INVESTOR

Brooke walked into the kitchen after school and casually dropped a question that made me realize everything we'd been teaching had finally clicked. She said, "Dad, with all the electric vehicle growth happening, shouldn't we own some Tesla stock? Or maybe the companies that make the batteries?"

She was sixteen and analyzing market trends over an after-school snack like she was discussing weekend plans.

But what struck me wasn't her investment insight—it was the word "we." Three years of financial education had created something unexpected: a teenager who saw wealth building as collaboration, not consumption.

THE SHIFT FROM ENTITLEMENT TO OWNERSHIP

Her language tells the story. A much younger Brooke had once said, "When I'm rich, I'll buy...". Now, she says "When I'm managing family investments, I want to focus on..."

She approaches money decisions like my most disciplined clients by evaluating trade-offs, considering long-term impact, and asking about value creation instead of just acquisition.

Her part-time job watching kids at the after-school program has taught her that money flows from solving problems for others. Her budget management has shown her that choices have consequences. The family investment discussions have revealed that wealth building requires patience and strategy, not luck and wishful thinking.

THE UNEXPECTED RESULT

Financial education hasn't created anxiety about money, and instead it has created capability with money. When Brooke eventually inherits wealth, she won't be inheriting a burden she's unprepared to handle. She'll be inheriting tools she already knows how to use.

THE ESTATE PLAN THAT ACTUALLY WORKS

Meanwhile, my father's estate plan has proven its worth through smaller tests.

When he was hospitalized for three weeks last year, I was able to manage every aspect of his financial life seamlessly by paying his bills, making investment decisions, and handling business operations because the proper documents were in place.

When one of his tenants sued for a slip-and-fall injury, the liability was contained to that specific property's LLC, protecting his other assets.

When tax law changes created new planning opportunities, his flexible trust structure allowed us to adapt without starting over.

"The plan isn't perfect," he told me recently. "But it's working. And more importantly, you're prepared to make it work better."

THE RIPPLE EFFECT: WHY THIS MATTERS BEYOND OUR FAMILY

The impact of that 2:47 AM conversation extends far beyond our family's financial security.

In my practice, I now require comprehensive legacy planning for every client with substantial assets. I've seen too many families destroyed by wealth that wasn't properly prepared or protected.

The Martinez Family Revival: After Carlos died without proper planning, he left his children to fight over a chaotic estate. I helped them create the family governance system he never built. Two years later, they are working together to rebuild and expand what he started.

The Johnson Legacy System: This successful family used our planning approach to transition leadership across three generations, allowing them to grow from 12 to 31 stores.

The Chen Family Constitution: David Chen's widow used the painful lessons from his death to create comprehensive planning for her children to ensure they would never face the chaos she experienced.

The Question That Started It All

"Why not us?"

That is the question my father asked me as dawn broke over our document-covered kitchen table.

"Why shouldn't our family be among the 10% that successfully transfers wealth across generations? Why shouldn't Brooke's children and grandchildren benefit from what we're building today? Why shouldn't our family create a legacy that lasts for centuries instead of disappearing in decades?"

The answer, I learned, isn't about having more money or smarter investments or better legal documents.

It is about understanding that **true wealth transfer is not financial—it is educational.**

It is about preparing people, not just preparing paperwork.

It is about creating systems that develop character, not just conserve capital.

It is about building families that can handle wealth, not just families that can accumulate it.

YOUR 2:47 AM MOMENT

You don't need to wait for a crisis call in the middle of the night to start this conversation with your family.

You don't need to wait until you have millions of dollars or dozens of properties or complex business structures.

You need to start now, with whatever you have, wherever you are, because the habits and systems that preserve wealth take time to develop.

The immediate actions you can take today:

1. **Calculate your potential estate tax liability**, even if it's currently zero, plan for growth.
2. **Review and update all beneficiary designations** on every account you own.
3. **Create or update basic estate documents** like wills, powers of attorney, healthcare. directives
4. **Start family financial conversations** with age-appropriate transparency.

5. **Establish values-based financial decision-making** in your household.

THIS IS THE CHOICE THAT WILL DEFINE LEGACIES.

Will you build wealth that empowers your family for generations? Will you accumulate assets that burden them with problems they are unprepared to solve?

Will you be part of the 10% that successfully transfers wealth and wisdom, or part of the 90% that loses everything within three generations?

Will you wait for your own 2:47 AM crisis call, or will you create the systems that make such calls unnecessary?

The documents are waiting to be drafted.

The conversations are waiting to be started.

The legacy is waiting to be built.

The only question remaining is the one that started it all:

Why not you? Why not your family? Why not now?

CHAPTER 11

The Inheritance Trap —Why Money Destroys More Families Than It Saves

THE ESTATE PLANNING LESSON HIDING IN PLAIN SIGHT

Patricia Williams sat across from me in my office, methodically organizing documents into neat piles like she was preparing for surgery. Investment statements. Insurance policies. Bank records. Real estate deeds. The paper trail of a successful life.

"Tom and I built all this together," she said, with her voice steady but her hands trembling as she touched each document. "Seven-figure retirement accounts. The house in Short Hills. College funds for both kids. We did everything right, didn't we?"

I nodded, recognizing the familiar pattern. Tom and Patricia Williams looked like textbook wealth builders from the outside. Successful careers, smart investments, growing net worth year after year. They'd followed every financial planning rule in the book.

But sitting there in my office eighteen months after Tom's sudden death, surrounded by the remnants of their financial life, Patricia was learning a devastating truth: **building wealth and protecting wealth require completely different skill sets.**

"The money is all still there," Patricia continued, her voice growing smaller. "But getting to it has been a nightmare. Bank accounts were frozen for months. The investment accounts are still tied up in probate. Tom's business partnership dissolved into legal warfare. And the kids..." she paused, fighting back tears. "The kids keep asking why Daddy's money is causing so many problems."

THE PERFECT LIFE THAT WASN'T PROTECTED

Tom Williams had been the epitome of the successful Summer investor. At fifty-two, he was earning high six figures in medical device sales, maximizing his 401(k) contributions, and systematically building wealth across multiple accounts. His investment portfolio was sophisticated, his insurance coverage was substantial, and his tax planning was aggressive.

But Tom had made one catastrophic assumption: he thought he had time to "get his affairs in order" later.

Three weeks before his heart attack, Tom had mentioned to Patricia that they needed to "update some paperwork" and "maybe see an estate planning attorney." He'd scheduled an appointment for the Monday after he died.

"Tom was brilliant about growing money," Patricia said, staring at the stack of statements. "But he never planned for what would happen to that money if he wasn't here to manage it."

THE PAPER TRAIL OF UNFINISHED BUSINESS

As Patricia walked me through Tom's financial landscape, the magnitude of his oversight became clear:

Investment accounts at five different firms because Tom had chased promotional rates and signup bonuses without considering consolidation.

Business partnership agreements with clauses Patricia couldn't understand but that would determine whether she received $200,000 or $500,000 from Tom's ownership stake.

Life insurance policies with conflicting beneficiary designations—one naming Patricia, another naming "the estate," triggering unnecessary taxes and probate delays.

Real estate holdings in multiple entities that Tom had created for tax optimization but never explained to Patricia.

A 401(k) account that still listed Tom's college girlfriend as beneficiary because he'd never updated the paperwork after their marriage.

"I lived with this man for twenty-two years," Patricia said, her voice filled with bitter discovery. "But I had no idea how complicated our financial life had become."

THE $700,000 LESSON

Over the next eighteen months, I watched Patricia's inheritance get consumed by the machinery of an unprepared estate:

$180,000 vanished into probate costs because assets weren't properly titled for immediate transfer.

$95,000 disappeared in unnecessary estate taxes due to lack of basic planning strategies.

$240,000 was lost when Tom's business partnership dissolved under terms that favored his surviving partners.

$130,000 evaporated in family legal fees as relatives fought over unclear inheritance instructions.

$55,000 in opportunity costs from investment accounts sitting idle during legal proceedings.

Tom's careful wealth building had created a $1.3 million estate. Patricia ultimately gained access to $595,000. Nearly 55% of Tom's life's work disappeared into a system designed to protect people who hadn't protected themselves.

But the financial losses were secondary to the emotional devastation. Patricia spent two years in courtrooms instead of grieving. Tom's children learned to associate their father's memory with family conflict instead of family security. Relationships with extended family never recovered from the legal battles.

"I used to be proud of what Tom and I built together," Patricia told me at our final meeting. "Now I warn other couples not to make the same mistakes we did."

THE ONE-HOUR SOLUTION THAT COULD HAVE SAVED EVERYTHING

The tragedy of Tom's estate wasn't the market crash that triggered his panic about wealth preservation—it was the absence of basic protection that would have cost less than $5,000 and taken less than one afternoon to implement.

A revocable living trust would have avoided probate entirely. **Updated beneficiary designations** would have eliminated the ex-girlfriend complication. **A buy-sell agreement** would have protected his business partnership value. **Powers of attorney** would have given Patricia immediate access to manage accounts during crisis.

These aren't complex strategies reserved for the ultra-wealthy. They're basic protection tools that every Summer investor should have in place.

Patricia's nightmare became my wake-up call. I now require estate planning foundation as part of every Summer season investment strategy, not as an optional add-on for "later."

Because in wealth building, later often becomes never. And never becomes a family tragedy that could have been easily prevented.

The Three Phases of Family Wealth Destruction

After helping dozens of families navigate similar crises, I've identified three predictable phases that turn inherited wealth from opportunity into agony.

Patricia's family experienced all three phases with devastating precision.

Phase 1: The Shock - When Success Becomes Complexity

The first indication that Tom's death would create financial chaos came within 48 hours, when Patricia tried to access their joint checking account to pay for funeral expenses.

"I'm sorry, Mrs. Williams," the bank representative said with practiced sympathy. "This account requires both signatures for withdrawals over $500. We'll need a death certificate and probate authorization to release funds."

What Patricia didn't know was that Tom had been steadily moving money into individual accounts for "tax optimization" purposes—a strategy their accountant had recommended but never fully explained to her.

Over the next month, Patricia discovered,

Fourteen different financial accounts scattered across six institutions, each with different access requirements and legal complications.

Three business entities she'd never heard of, including an LLC that owned their vacation rental property and an S-Corp that held Tom's consulting income.

Two life insurance policies with conflicting beneficiary designations—one naming Patricia, and another naming "the estate," which would trigger unnecessary taxes and delays.

Investment accounts at five different firms because Tom had chased promotional rates and signup bonuses without considering consolidation.

A complex partnership agreement for his medical device business that included clauses Patricia couldn't understand but that would determine whether she received $200,000 or $500,000 from Tom's share.

"I felt like I was married to a stranger," Patricia told me, her voice bitter with the discovery. "Twenty-two years together, and I had no idea how complicated our financial life had become."

Phase 2: The Split - When Grief Becomes Greed

The family conflicts began innocuously enough with disagreements about funeral arrangements that escalated into arguments about their new wealth.

Tom's brother Marcus believed Patricia was "hiding assets" because the estate seemed smaller than Tom's lifestyle had suggested. Tom's parents thought Patricia should use life insurance proceeds to pay off the mortgage immediately rather than investing for the children's education.

But the real explosion came when they discovered Tom's biggest financial mistake: a $500,000 401(k) account that still listed his college girlfriend as beneficiary.

"That money belongs to our children," Patricia insisted during a heated family meeting. "Tom just forgot to update the paperwork."

"The law is the law," Marcus shot back. "If Tom wanted Patricia to have that money, he would have changed the beneficiary. Maybe there's a reason he didn't."

The accusation hung in the air like poison gas. Within days, Marcus had hired his own attorney to "protect Tom's true intentions." Tom's parents followed suit, claiming Patricia was "financially irresponsible" and demanding oversight of their grandchildren's inheritance.

Three lawyers. Three interpretations of Tom's wishes. Three mounting piles of legal bills that grew larger every month.

"We went from being a family to being adversaries," Patricia told me, tears streaming down her face. "And the money—the money that Tom worked so hard to provide for us—became the weapon we used to destroy each other."

Phase 3: The Surrender - When Winning Becomes Losing

Eighteen months after Tom's death, Patricia sat in my office with the final settlement agreement, a document that represented the collapse of her family's financial future.

To end the legal warfare, she had agreed to:

- Give Tom's brother 20% of the estate value to drop his claims
- Establish a trust controlled by Tom's parents for the children's inheritance
- Pay $180,000 in combined legal fees for all parties
- Accept the ex-girlfriend's claim to the $500,000 401(k)

"I just wanted it to be over," Patricia said, signing the papers with shaking hands. "I couldn't fight anymore. The kids were asking why Grandma and Uncle Marcus hated us. I was spending more time with lawyers than with my children."

The settlement gave Patricia immediate access to about $400,000, which was less than one-third of what Tom had actually built for his family.

But the real tragedy was not financial—it was relational. Patricia's children would grow up estranged from their father's family. Tom's parents would never recover their relationship with their daughter-in-law. Marcus would carry the guilt of his accusations for the rest of his life.

All because a successful man thought estate planning could wait until he was "older."

THE ANATOMY OF WEALTH DESTRUCTION

Patricia's story is not unique. It follows a pattern I have seen repeated in dozens of families:

The Success Trap: People who are competent at building wealth often believe they are competent at protecting it, even though these require completely different skill sets.

The Time Illusion: Young, healthy, successful people consistently overestimate how much time they have to «get their affairs in order.»

The Complexity Creep: As wealth grows, financial structures become more complex, but most people don't invest proportionally in systems to manage that complexity.

The Communication Void: Families rarely discuss wealth openly, leaving family members unprepared for the responsibilities that inheritance brings.

The Professional Procrastination: People delay working with estate planning attorneys because the process forces them to confront their own mortality.

THE LEGACY DESTROYER: UNPREPARED HEIRS

But even families that avoid Patricia's nightmare often fall into a more subtle trap by creating heirs who are unprepared for the wealth they inherit.

THE MARTINEZ FAMILY MELTDOWN

Carlos Martinez spent thirty years building a million-dollar landscaping business from a single pickup truck. He owned rental properties, had substantial investment accounts, and constantly talked about leaving his children "set for life."

But Carlos made the classic mistake that destroys generational wealth: he built assets without building character.

His three children—Jennifer, Miguel, and Sofia—had been shielded from financial responsibility their entire lives. Carlos paid for everything: cars, college, apartments, credit card bills, and even his grandchildren's expenses. He thought he was being generous. Instead, he was creating financial dependents.

When Carlos died suddenly of a heart attack at sixty-two, his children inherited substantial wealth but lacked the wisdom to manage it.

THE DESTRUCTION TIMELINE

Year 1: Jennifer used her inheritance to quit her job and «find herself» through expensive travel and shopping sprees.

Year 2: Miguel invested heavily in cryptocurrency after reading online forums, losing 80% of his inheritance when the market crashed.

Year 3: Sofia lent money to friends and family members for various «business opportunities,» most of which failed.

Year 4: The siblings began fighting over the remaining family assets, hiring lawyers to force liquidation of the business and properties.

Year 5: Carlos' million-dollar legacy had been reduced to less than $200,000 divided among three children, who were now financially dependent on their spouses and bitter toward each other.

"Dad thought he was protecting us by handling everything," Jennifer told me during a painful family meeting. "Instead, he left us completely unprepared for the responsibility he was giving us."

THE PREPARATION DEFICIT

This pattern repeats across socioeconomic levels because wealthy parents make the same fundamental error: they focus on accumulating assets for their children instead of developing capabilities in their children.

Research from the Williams Group, a family wealth consulting firm, identifies the primary causes of inherited wealth destruction:

60% - Breakdown in communication and trust

25% - Unprepared heirs

10% - Lack of family mission

5% - All other factors (taxes, legal issues, economic conditions)

Notice what's NOT on that list: market crashes, economic downturns, or "unlucky" investments. **95% of wealth destruction is caused by human factors that proper planning can address.**

THE ANTIDOTE: INTENTIONAL WEALTH TRANSFER

The families that successfully transfer wealth across generations share common characteristics that distinguish them from those who fail:

They educate before they accumulate. They develop character before they distribute assets. They create systems before they create inheritances. They build capabilities before they build trust funds.

THE JOHNSON FAMILY: HARDWARE STORE TEST THAT BUILT CHARACTER

The first time I met Robert Johnson, he was standing in the lumber aisle of his flagship hardware store, watching his eighteen-year-old son Michael ring up a customer's purchase.

"See that?" Robert whispered, nodding towards Michael. "He has no idea that every transaction teaches him something about people, profit, and patience. He thinks he's just working a summer job."

Robert owned twelve hardware stores across the Midwest. He wasn't just building a retail empire he was building his children's character. And he had a radical theory about inheritance that would either create a dynasty or destroy his relationship with his children.

"My kids will inherit these stores over my dead body," Robert said with a mischievous grin. "They'll have to earn them while I'm alive to see it happen."

THE SUMMER THAT SHOCKED EVERYONE

When Michael turned sixteen, he expected to be handed a management position at the family stores. Instead, Robert sent him to work at Home Depot.

"You want me to work for the competition?" Michael asked, his teenage indignation barely contained.

"I want you to understand what we're competing against," Robert replied. "And I want you to learn what good customer service looks like when nobody knows you're the boss's son."

Michael spent two summers stocking shelves, loading lumber, and dealing with contractors who treated teenage employees as if they were disposable labor. He learned that retail was harder than it looked, that the customers could be brutal, and earning respect had nothing to do with last names.

"I hated my father that first summer," Michael told me years later. "All my friends were working cushy jobs at their family businesses, and I was getting yelled at by strangers for $8.50 an hour."

But something shifted during his second summer at Home Depot. Michael began noticing inefficiencies and suggesting improvements to managers. He soon began developing opinions about what Johnson Hardware could do better.

"When I finally came back to work for Dad, I wasn't just grateful for the job," Michael reflected. "I was angry about how much better we could be doing."

THE VETERINARIAN PLOT TWIST

Robert's middle child, Sarah, dropped a bomb at Sunday dinner when she turned twenty: "Dad, I don't want anything to do with hardware stores. I want to be a veterinarian."

The table went silent. Robert's wife looked nervous. Michael and Tommy waited for the explosion.

Instead, Robert smiled. "Tell me about your business plan."

"My what?"

"Your business plan. How are you going to build a veterinary practice that serves people the way our hardware stores do? What will make your clinic different? How will you finance it? What's your five-year growth strategy?"

Sarah stared at her father like he'd started speaking Mandarin.

"Being a Johnson doesn't mean selling hammers," Robert explained. "It means building something meaningful that serves your community. If you're going to be a vet, you're going to be the best vet in the state. And you're going to approach it like the entrepreneur you are."

Today, Sarah owns the largest veterinary clinic in three counties. Robert provided her business mentorship and startup capital and treated her practice like another Johnson family enterprise. Her clinic employs sixteen people and anchors the family's healthcare real estate investments.

THE CREATIVE SON'S BUSINESS REVOLUTION

Tommy was the family wildcard. He is artistic, dreamy, and seemingly uninterested in business. Robert worried he was raising two entrepreneurs and one starving artist.

At twenty-eight, Tommy had completed college with business and art double majors. Soon after, he requested a family meeting to present what he called "The Johnson Hardware Revolution."

"We're thinking too small," Tommy announced, unveiling designs and spreadsheets that made his practical siblings' heads spin. "These stores are positioned perfectly for the DIY economy, but we're stuck in 1995. We need e-commerce, home renovation services, and design consultation."

Tommy's artistic eye saw opportunities his business-minded brothers had missed. His e-commerce platform made Johnson Hardware accessible to customers three states away.

His design services turned one-time shoppers into lifetime clients planning major home projects.

"Dad always said I was the creative one," Tommy laughed during our recent business review. "Turns out creativity applied to business is just innovation with profit margins."

Today, Tommy's digital innovations generate 40% of Johnson Hardware's revenue.

THE TWENTY-YEAR RESULTS

Before Robert died at seventy-three, he had gotten the opportunity to witness something most business founders never see: his children working together by choice, not obligation.

Michael runs operations with the confidence he developed after working at Home Dept. Sarah's veterinary empire anchors the family's healthcare investments. Tommy's innovations keep the business competitive in an Amazon world.

The hardware stores have grown from 12 locations to 31, but that's not the real success story. The real success is three siblings who respect each other's contributions, trust each other's judgment, and choose to work together because collaboration amplifies their individual strengths.

"We don't have family business meetings," Michael explained recently. "We have business family meetings. The difference is that we're choosing to build something together instead of being forced to manage something we inherited."

At Robert's funeral, his longtime banker said something that captured his genius. He stated, "Robert didn't raise kids who inherited a business. He raised business owners who happened to be his kids."

That distinction made all the difference. Inherited wealth creates entitled heirs. Earned responsibility creates wealth creators.

Robert understood that the greatest tool isn't money, it's the ability to create money. He knew he had to help his children develop the character and judgement to handle it wisely.

THE DEVELOPMENT VS. DISTRIBUTION CHOICE

Every parent building wealth faces a fundamental choice: **Will you focus on distributing assets or developing people?**

Most choose distribution because it feels like love. It is incredibly fulfilling to be able to provide for your children's material needs and removing financial obstacles from their lives to ensure they never experience the struggles you had faced.

On the contrary, it is crucial to remember that distribution without development creates entitled adults who consume wealth rather than creating it.

Development focuses on building capabilities:

- Financial literacy and investment knowledge
- Work ethic and value creation skills
- Character traits like discipline and integrity
- Leadership abilities and decision-making judgment
- Understanding of responsibility and stewardship

Distribution focuses on providing assets:

- Trust funds and inheritance accounts
- Paid education and living expenses
- Gifts of real estate or business ownership

- Access to family investment accounts
- Lifestyle funding without earning requirements

The families that succeed long-term choose development first, distribution second.

BUILDING ANTI-FRAGILE HEIRS

The goal is not to make inheritance easy. It is to make heirs capable of handling difficulty.

Financial Anti-Fragility means your children become stronger and more capable when they face financial challenges, rather than being destroyed by them.

To ensure your children become anti-fragile heirs, follow the framework below.

THE ANTI-FRAGILITY DEVELOPMENT FRAMEWORK

Controlled Failure: Create situations where children can make mistakes and experience consequences while the stakes are manageable.

Graduated Responsibility: Increase financial responsibility gradually as children demonstrate competence at lower levels.

Values Integration: Connect money decisions to family values and larger purpose beyond personal consumption.

Mentorship Networks: Provide access to successful people outside the family who can teach and challenge your children.

Meaningful Work: Require children to create value for others before they can access family wealth.

THE INHERITANCE READINESS ASSESSMENT

Before transferring substantial wealth to the next generation, successful families evaluate their heir readiness across the following standards,

Financial Competence

- Can they create and stick to a budget?
- Do they understand basic investment principles?
- Have they demonstrated the ability to earn money independently?
- Can they distinguish between assets and liabilities?

Character Development

- Do they treat money as a tool or as an identity?
- Are they generous with their time and resources?
- Do they take responsibility for their mistakes?
- Are they motivated by contribution or consumption?

Relationship Skills

- Can they work effectively with others?
- Do they handle conflict constructively?
- Are they capable of leading and following appropriately?
- Do they maintain healthy relationships across different social contexts?

Values Alignment

- Do their actions reflect stated family values?
- Are they motivated by purposes larger than personal pleasure?
- Do they understand their responsibility to future generations?
- Are they committed to using wealth for positive impact?

Vision and Purpose

- Do they have clear goals for their own lives?
- Can they articulate how wealth fits into their larger purpose?
- Are they prepared to be stewards rather than just consumers?
- Do they understand their role in continuing family legacy?

THE CONVERSATION FRAMEWORK

Successful wealth transfer requires ongoing family conversations about money, values, and responsibility. These conversations should evolve as the children mature. Make sure to ask them these questions and have conversations that cover these topics,

Ages 8-12: Foundation Conversations

- "How is money a tool that helps families create choices and help others?"

- "Why do you believe our family has been successful?"
    - ◊ Emphasize that your family has worked hard and treats people well!
- "How can we use our privileges wisely? What responsibilities come along with privilege?"

Ages 13-17: Development Conversations

- "You will likely inherit substantial resources someday, which means you need to prepare yourself to handle that responsibility..."
- "We expect you to become financially capable before you become financially dependent."
- "How are you going to use your inheritance? How will you prepare yourself for the future?"

Ages 18-25: Preparation Conversations

- "Here's specifically what you might inherit and when that might happen..."
- "Here are our expectations for your education, work experience, and character development..."
- "Here's how you can begin participating in family financial decisions..."

Ages 25+: Partnership Conversations

- "You're now ready to take on increasing responsibility for family wealth management"

- "Help us evaluate and improve our wealth transfer systems"
- "Begin preparing the next generation for their eventual responsibilities"

WHAT HAPPENS NEXT IS UP TO YOU

Patricia Williams sits in my office today, five years after Tom's death, helping other families avoid the nightmare she experienced. She's become one of my most effective advocates for proper planning—not because she's a natural salesperson, but because her story carries the weight of lived consequences.

"I tell people that losing Tom was devastating enough," she says. "But losing half his wealth to preventable chaos made the grief unbearable. No family should go through what we did."

Your next step isn't complex: Schedule an estate planning consultation this month. Not when you feel ready. Not when you have "enough" wealth to make it worthwhile. This month.

Because the families who successfully transfer wealth across generations share one characteristic: they plan while they're healthy, thinking clearly, and have time to build systems properly.

The inheritance trap isn't about market crashes or economic downturns. It's about smart people who assume they have more time than they actually do.

Patricia learned that assumption costs families everything. You don't have to.

CHAPTER 12

The Legacy Code, Designing Wealth That Lasts Centuries

THE DOCUMENT THAT CHANGED EVERYTHING

The manila folder was labeled simply "FOR BROOKE - WHEN I'M GONE" in my father's handwriting. He handed it to me with shaking hands during what we both knew would be one of our last conversations.

"Open it," he said. His voice carried the weight of someone who had spent months crafting something he hoped would outlive him by generations.

Inside was a document unlike anything I'd ever seen. It was part financial plan, part family constitution, and part love letter to the future. At the top, in bold letters, were words that would reshape how I understood legacy:

"THE RUIZ FAMILY LEGACY CODE - A Blueprint for Building Wealth That Survives and Thrives Across Generations"

"Mijo," my father said, watching me scan the pages, "what you're holding isn't just a plan for transferring money. It's the operating system for a family dynasty. Everything I learned about building wealth, protecting it, and passing it on—it's all here."

As I read deeper into the document, I realized this was not just estate planning. This was legacy architecture, which distinguished the difference between leaving wealth behind and leaving wisdom that compounds across centuries.

THE 200-YEAR VISION

My father's Legacy Code began with a vision that stretched far beyond his own lifetime:

"By the year 2224, the Ruiz family name will be synonymous with business excellence, community leadership, and philanthropic impact. Our descendants will look back on this generation as the foundation that launched centuries of prosperity, purpose, and positive influence on the world."

"Most people plan for their own retirement," he explained. "Rich people plan for their children's inheritance. But families that create lasting legacies plan for grandchildren they'll never meet."

The Legacy Code outlined specific systems for:

- Growing wealth across market cycles and economic changes

- Developing family members who could steward increasing responsibility
- Creating businesses and investments that would thrive for decades
- Building philanthropic impact that would compound over generations
- Maintaining family unity and shared purpose across time

"This isn't about the money we leave," my father said. "It's about the money-making capabilities we develop in every generation."

THE THREE-GENERATION TEST

Every element of the Legacy Code was designed to pass what my father called "The Three-Generation Test":

Generation 1, Builders: Creates the wealth and establishes the systems

Generation 2, Stewards: Preserves what was built while adapting to changing conditions

Generation 3, Multipliers: Expands the legacy while preparing the next cycle

"Most families fail because they optimize for Generation 1," my father explained. "They build wealth efficiently but don't create systems that survive the transition to new leadership."

The Legacy Code addressed this by creating structures that would become stronger, not weaker, as they passed through generational transitions.

THE FOUNDATION LAYER: VALUES THAT NEVER CHANGE

At the core of the Legacy Code were five immutable family values that would guide every financial decision across generations:

Value 1: Entrepreneurial Excellence

"We create value for others before capturing value for ourselves. Every generation must demonstrate the ability to build something meaningful."

Value 2: Educational Investment

"We invest in developing human capital as aggressively as we invest in financial capital. Learning and growth are non-negotiable family commitments."

Value 3: Community Stewardship

"We use our success to strengthen the communities that supported our growth. Giving back is not optional—it's essential to who we are."

Value 4: Generational Thinking

"We make decisions based on long-term impact, not short-term convenience. Every choice considers its effect on family members not yet born."

Value 5: Character Development

"We prioritize who we become over what we accumulate. Money without integrity is not wealth—it's a liability."

"These values aren't suggestions," my father said. "They're the DNA of our family's approach to money. Every investment decision, every business opportunity, every inheritance distribution should reflect these principles."

THE OPERATING LAYER: SYSTEMS THAT SCALE

Built on this foundation were five operational systems designed to function across generations:

System 1: The Family Investment Office

Instead of scattered individual accounts, the Legacy Code established a formal Family Investment Office that would,

- Consolidate investment management for efficiency and economies of scale
- Maintain disciplined asset allocation across all family portfolios
- Provide professional investment education for family members
- Create opportunities for family members to learn by managing smaller portfolios
- Generate superior returns through coordinated strategy and reduced fees

"Think of this like creating our own private mutual fund," my father explained. "But instead of outside investors, we're pooling family resources for better outcomes."

System 2: The Business Development Engine

Rather than simply investing in public markets, the Legacy Code created the system below for developing family business ventures,

- **Incubation Fund:** Capital specifically designated for new business development
- **Mentorship Network:** Relationships with successful entrepreneurs who could guide family ventures
- **Due Diligence Process:** Standardized evaluation criteria for business opportunities
- **Performance Metrics:** Clear success measures and exit strategies for each venture
- **Knowledge Transfer:** Documentation and sharing of lessons learned from both successes and failures

"Every generation should create at least one successful business," my father said. "Not just for the money, but for the skills and confidence that come from building something from nothing."

System 3: The Education Development Framework

Education in the Legacy Code goes far beyond traditional schooling.

- **Financial Literacy Curriculum:** Age-appropriate education about money, investing, and business
- **Leadership Development:** Opportunities to lead family projects and community initiatives
- **Global Perspective:** Travel and international experience requirements
- **Mentorship Relationships:** Formal pairing with successful non-family mentors

- **Real-World Testing:** Graduated responsibility for managing actual family assets

"We're not just funding education," my father explained. "We're systematically developing the capabilities each generation needs to handle increasing responsibility."

System 4: The Community Impact Platform

Philanthropic giving was structured as a family development tool.

- **Family Foundation:** Formal charitable entity with involvement opportunities for all family members
- **Impact Measurement:** Rigorous evaluation of charitable effectiveness and community outcomes
- **Service Requirements:** Mandatory volunteer service for family members at different life stages
- **Collaborative Decision-Making:** Family meetings to discuss and vote on major charitable commitments
- **Legacy Integration:** Charitable work connected to family business and investment activities

"Giving isn't just about helping others," my father said. "It's about teaching our family to think beyond ourselves and develop judgment about creating positive impact."

System 5: The Governance Framework

The most sophisticated element was a family governance system that would maintain unity and resolve conflicts swiftly.

- **Family Council:** Democratic body making major strategic decisions
- **Family Constitution:** Written document outlining roles, responsibilities, and decision-making processes
- **Conflict Resolution:** Structured mediation process for addressing disagreements
- **Performance Standards:** Clear expectations for family member behavior and contribution
- **Leadership Succession:** Formal process for transitioning authority to next generation

"Democracy works for countries, and it can work for families," my father said. "But only if you have clear rules and everyone agrees to follow them."

THE WEALTH MULTIPLICATION STRATEGY

The Legacy Code's approach to growing wealth was designed to work across decades and changing economic conditions.

Conservative Base (60% of portfolio): Broad market index funds, bonds, and real estate that would preserve purchasing power across generations

Growth Engine (30% of portfolio): More aggressive investments in emerging markets, growth companies, and family business ventures

Opportunity Fund (10% of portfolio): Capital reserved for exceptional opportunities that emerge during market downturns or economic dislocations

"The goal isn't to get rich quick," my father explained. "It's to get rich permanently. That requires balancing growth with preservation."

The multiplication strategy also included specific provisions for different economic environments,

Bull Markets: Systematic rebalancing to harvest gains and maintain target allocations.

Bear Markets: Opportunistic investing when quality assets become available at discount prices.

Inflationary Periods: Increased allocation to real assets and business ownership.

Deflationary Periods: Higher cash reserves and focus on debt reduction.

The Human Development Pipeline

The most innovative aspect of the Legacy Code was its systematic approach to preparing family members for wealth stewardship:

Ages 5-12: Foundation Building

- Financial literacy education through games and age-appropriate activities
- Exposure to family businesses and investment properties
- Community service and charitable giving participation
- Character development through responsibilities and consequences

Ages 13-18: Skill Development

- Part-time employment to understand the connection between work and compensation
- Formal financial education including budgeting, investing, and business fundamentals
- Leadership roles in school, community, or family projects
- Travel and cultural exposure to build global perspective

Ages 19-25: Capability Testing

- Independent employment or business venture with minimal family support
- College education with performance standards and practical application requirements
- Mentorship relationships with successful non-family professionals
- Graduated responsibility for managing small portions of family wealth

Ages 26-35: Integration and Leadership

- Eligibility for significant roles in family businesses or investment management
- Full participation in family governance and strategic decision-making

- Mentorship responsibilities for younger family members
- Leadership of major family initiatives or community projects

Ages 36+: Stewardship and Succession

- Senior leadership roles in family enterprises
- Primary responsibility for developing next generation
- Strategic oversight of family legacy preservation and growth
- Community leadership and philanthropic impact

"Each phase builds on the previous one," my father explained. "By the time someone is ready for significant responsibility, they've proven their capability at every level."

THE CRISIS MANAGEMENT PROTOCOL

The Legacy Code included detailed protocols for maintaining family unity during difficult periods:

Financial Crises: Procedures for preserving capital and maintaining family support during economic downturns

Family Conflicts: Structured mediation and resolution processes before problems escalate to legal warfare

Leadership Transitions: Clear succession planning that prevents power struggles and uncertainty

External Threats: Strategies for protecting family privacy and security as wealth increases

Generational Gaps: Systems for bridging differences in values and perspectives across age groups

"Every family faces crises," my father said. "The difference between families that survive and families that collapse is whether they have systems for handling crisis before it arrives."

THE LEGACY METRICS DASHBOARD

To ensure the Legacy Code was working, my father created a comprehensive measurement system:

Financial Metrics

- Net worth growth across all family members
- Investment returns compared to relevant benchmarks
- Business venture success rates and profitability
- Tax efficiency and estate planning optimization

Human Development Metrics

- Educational achievement and skill development
- Career success and leadership demonstration
- Financial responsibility and decision-making capability
- Character development and values alignment

Impact Metrics

- Community contributions and volunteer service
- Charitable giving effectiveness and outcomes
- Business practices and ethical standards
- Family unity and relationship quality

Legacy Preservation Metrics

- Knowledge transfer effectiveness across generations
- Family governance system performance
- Conflict resolution success rates
- Long-term vision alignment and progress

"What gets measured gets managed," my father said. "If we're serious about building a lasting legacy, we need to track whether our systems are actually working."

THE IMPLEMENTATION TIMELINE

The Legacy Code included a specific implementation timeline that would unfold over the first ten years:

Years 1-2: Foundation Building

- Establish family investment office and consolidate assets
- Create family foundation and begin coordinated charitable giving
- Draft family constitution and governance documents

- Begin systematic financial education for younger family members

Years 3-5: System Development

- Launch first family business development project
- Implement formal mentorship and development programs
- Establish performance measurement and reporting systems
- Create crisis management and conflict resolution protocols

Years 6-10: Integration and Optimization

- Transition leadership responsibilities to next generation
- Evaluate and refine all Legacy Code systems based on results
- Expand community impact and philanthropic effectiveness
- Prepare for next generational transition

"This isn't something you build overnight," my father warned. "But every month you delay starting is a month stolen from your family's future."

THE BROOKE TEST: MAKING IT PERSONAL

As I finished reading the Legacy Code, my father asked me a question that made everything personal:

"What do you want Brooke's children to know about money, work, and responsibility?"

I thought about my sixteen-year-old daughter, already showing signs of the entrepreneurial spirit and community consciousness that the Legacy Code was designed to develop.

"I want them to see wealth as responsibility, not privilege," I said slowly. "I want them to understand that money is a tool for creating value and helping others. I want them to be capable of building their own success while being grateful for the foundation we're providing."

"Then you need to start implementing these systems now," my father said. "Not when Brooke graduates college. Not when she gets married. Not when she has children of her own. Now, while her understanding of money and family and responsibility is still forming."

THE RUIZ FAMILY LEGACY CODE IMPLEMENTATION

Over the past three years, we've been systematically implementing the Legacy Code systems:

Family Investment Office: We consolidated scattered accounts and established coordinated investment management, reducing fees, and improving returns.

Education Framework: We established formal financial education milestones and connected them to increasing privileges and responsibilities.

Community Impact: Our family foundation has donated to local education initiatives, while involving Brooke in the selection and evaluation process.

Governance System: We hold quarterly family meetings to discuss financial decisions, review progress, and address any concerns or conflicts.

The results have been remarkable both financially and in terms of family unity.

THE COMPOUND EFFECT OF LEGACY THINKING

The most powerful aspect of the Legacy Code is how all the systems work together to create compound growth across multiple dimensions:

Financial Compounding: Money grows through systematic investment and business development

Knowledge Compounding: Each generation builds on the previous generation's experience and wisdom

Network Compounding: Family relationships and business connections expand exponentially over time

Impact Compounding: Community contributions and charitable effectiveness multiply across generations

"You know what separates the families who keep wealth from those who lose it?" my father asked during our final planning session. "The ones who succeed assume the next generation will make mistakes, so they build systems that make good decisions easier than bad ones."

YOUR LEGACY CODE: DESIGN QUESTIONS

Creating your own Legacy Code requires answering fundamental questions about your family's purpose and systems:

Values Foundation

- What principles should guide every generation's financial decisions?
- How do you want your family to be remembered in your community?
- What character traits are non-negotiable for family members?

Wealth Strategy

- How will you grow wealth across different economic cycles?
- What's your approach to balancing preservation with growth?
- How will you create multiple income streams across generations?

Human Development

- What capabilities must each generation develop?
- How will you prepare family members for increasing responsibility?
- What education and experience requirements will you establish?

Governance Structure

- How will major family decisions be made?
- What processes will you use to resolve conflicts?
- How will leadership transition from one generation to the next?

Impact Mission

- How will your family contribute to community and society?
- What legacy do you want to create beyond financial wealth?
- How will you measure success across multiple generations?

YOUR LEGACY CODE IMPLEMENTATION PLAN

This system takes several years to develop. The first year requires the most steps, but is extremely worth the time.

Year 1, Month 1-3: Foundation Assessment

- Define your family's core values and long-term vision
- Evaluate current wealth management and estate planning structures
- Assess family members' current preparation levels
- Identify gaps between your current approach and legacy thinking

Year 1, Month 4-6: System Design

- Create your family constitution and governance framework

- Establish consolidated investment management approach
- Design human development pipeline for each family member
- Plan community impact and philanthropic strategy

Year 1, Month 7-12: Implementation Beginning

- Launch family governance and communication systems
- Begin consolidated wealth management and business development
- Start systematic education and development programs
- Establish measurement and evaluation systems

Years 2-5: System Optimization

- Refine governance and decision-making processes based on experience
- Expand business development and investment opportunities
- Advance family member development and responsibility levels
- Evaluate and improve community impact effectiveness

Years 6-10: Legacy Acceleration

- Transition increasing responsibility to next generation
- Create formal succession and leadership development plans
- Establish permanent systems for ongoing legacy preservation
- Begin preparing for multi-generational wealth transfer

THE CHOICE THAT ECHOES THROUGH CENTURIES

As my father handed me his Legacy Code three years ago, he said something that changed how I thought about everything we had built.

"Son, the money is just the beginning. What we're really creating is a family culture that will outlive both of us. A way of thinking about wealth and responsibility that will guide decisions long after we're gone."

The Legacy Code is not just about estate planning or investment management or family governance. It is about designing a family culture that creates wealth-building capabilities in every generation.

It is about the choice between leaving money and leaving systems.

Between creating wealth and creating wealth creators.

Between building for one generation and building for many.

The code is waiting to be written. The systems are waiting to be built. The legacy is waiting to be designed.

The only question is, will you design your family's legacy intentionally? Or will you leave it to chance?

Why not your family? Why not a legacy that lasts for centuries? Why not starting today?

CHAPTER 13

Building Your Dynasty —The Implementation Blueprint

THE FAMILY MEETING THAT ALMOST DIDN'T HAPPEN

David Chen stared at the conference room he'd reserved at the Marriott, second-guessing everything. Twelve family members were supposed to arrive in an hour for what he'd called "an important family discussion." But looking at the flip charts and handouts he'd prepared, he wondered if he was about to destroy his family's relationships over spreadsheets and statistics.

His wife, Jennifer, walked in carrying coffee and noticed his expression. "Having doubts?" she asked.

"What if they think I've lost my mind?" David asked, gesturing at his carefully prepared materials. "What if they walk out? What if this destroys everything instead of protecting it?"

Jennifer sat down across from him. "What if it works?"

THE QUESTION THAT STARTED EVERYTHING

The meeting began awkwardly. David's 78-year-old father sat stiffly in his chair, clearly uncomfortable with the formal setting. His siblings, Michelle and Peter, exchanged skeptical glances. The teenagers looked up from their phones long enough to wonder why they were there.

"I know this feels strange," David began, his voice shakier than he'd planned. "But I've been losing sleep over something, and I need your help."

He pulled out a single sheet of paper, not a presentation slide, just a handwritten note.

"Last month, I attended the funeral of a business colleague. His family was wealthy—multiple millions. But within eighteen months of his death, his children were all involved in lawsuits, his business was liquidated for pennies on the dollar, and his grandchildren will grow up hearing stories about how money destroyed their family."

David's father leaned forward. This wasn't about theories or frameworks. This was about real consequences.

"That could be us," David continued. "We've been successful as individuals, but we've never thought about what happens to our success when we're gone."

THE UNCOMFORTABLE TRUTH

Michelle was the first to speak: "David, we're not even that wealthy. This feels a bit dramatic."

"Are we not?" David asked. He'd prepared for this moment. "Dad's accumulated $2.1 million in retirement savings and real estate. I've built a $3.8 million business and investment portfolio. Peter, your medical practice and investments are worth what—$1.6 million? Michelle, your accounting firm and real estate put you around $1.2 million."

The room went quiet as family members did the mental math.

"Together, we control nearly $9 million," David said. "But we operate like strangers who happen to share holidays. We have no coordination, no planning, no systems. If something happens to any of us tomorrow, chaos will follow."

THE STORY THAT HIT HOME

David's teenage daughter Sarah broke the uncomfortable silence: "What happened to your friend's family? Specifically?". David had hoped someone would ask.

He explained, "Their dad died without updating his business partnership agreement. His partners were able to buy out his share at book value instead of fair market value—a difference of $800,000. His personal investments were scattered across different accounts with outdated beneficiaries. His ex-business partner from ten years ago inherited his largest retirement account because he never changed the paperwork."

"But the worst part," David continued, his voice growing quiet, "was watching his children blame each other. His daughter accused his son of hiding assets. His son accused his daughter of manipulating their father before he died. They spent two years in court and haven't spoken since."

Peter shifted uncomfortably. "So, what are you proposing?"

THE CHOICE, NOT THE SYSTEM

"I'm proposing that we make a choice," David said. "We can continue operating as individuals who happen to be related, or we can start operating as a family that builds wealth together."

He put away his prepared materials. This conversation was too important for flip charts.

"I don't want to control anyone's money or business decisions," David continued. "But I think we should coordinate our planning so that we're protecting each other instead of accidentally creating problems for each other."

David's father spoke for the first time: "What would that look like?"

"I don't know yet," David admitted. "That's why I need everyone here. We figure it out together, or we don't do it at all."

THE MOMENT OF TRUTH

For the next three hours, the conversation flowed between practical concerns and deeper fears. Michelle worried about losing autonomy over her business. Peter questioned whether coordination might complicate their taxes. The teenagers wondered if this was about controlling their inheritance.

But gradually, something shifted. Stories emerged about business opportunities that might benefit multiple family members. Questions arose about whether they were all using the best financial advisors. Someone mentioned that maybe they should be thinking about charitable giving as a family activity.

By the end of the meeting, they hadn't solved anything. But they'd agreed to something more important: the idea they wanted to solve it together.

"This isn't about building some corporate family structure," David said as they wrapped up. "It's about making sure our individual success doesn't accidentally become our family's failure."

THE SMALL STEPS THAT CREATED BIG CHANGES

SIX MONTHS LATER: THE RENTAL PROPERTY DECISION

The Chen family's first test came when Peter wanted to sell a rental property he'd inherited from his grandfather. Under the old approach, he would have made the decision alone. Under their new family coordination, he brought it to the quarterly family call.

"I'm thinking of selling Grandpa's duplex," Peter announced. "The tenants are moving out, and I don't want to deal with finding new ones."

David saw opportunity where Peter saw hassle. "What if we kept it but managed it differently? Michelle's accounting firm handles several rental properties. I know contractors who could renovate it. We could turn it into a family investment instead of Peter's headache."

Three months later, the renovated duplex was generating 40% more rental income than before. Peter kept ownership but gained family support for management. David's contractor got a profitable project. Michelle's firm gained a new client.

"We turned one person's problem into everyone's opportunity," Michelle reflected.

YEAR ONE: THE BUSINESS CONNECTION

The coordination created unexpected synergies. Peter's medical practice needed a new accounting system. Michelle's firm specialized in healthcare accounting. David's tech background helped design a custom solution that Michelle could offer to other medical clients.

"We went from being siblings who happened to have businesses to being business owners who happened to be siblings," Peter observed. "The difference is that now we look for ways to help each other succeed."

YEAR TWO: THE NEXT GENERATION CONVERSATION

David's son, Michael, was struggling to choose between college majors. Instead of individual advice, he got family perspective. Peter shared insights about healthcare career, Michelle discussed business and accounting paths, and David talked about entrepreneurship and technology.

"Having multiple successful adults invested in my future felt different than just having my parents give advice," Michael said. "It made me realize that family success creates more opportunities for everyone."

THE UNEXPECTED OUTCOMES

FINANCIAL RESULTS WITHOUT FINANCIAL FOCUS

Three years after that awkward conference room meeting, the Chen family had achieved something remarkable: they'd improved their financial outcomes by focusing on relationships instead of returns.

Coordination Benefits

- Shared professional services reduced everyone's costs
- Cross-referrals grew everyone's businesses
- Bulk purchasing power on insurance and investments
- Coordinated tax planning saved the family over $40,000 annually
- Estate planning alignment eliminated potential conflicts

Individual Growth

- David's business expanded into healthcare technology
- Peter's practice grew through Michelle's referral network
- Michelle's firm developed healthcare specialization
- The next generation gained multiple mentors and career guidance

THE FOUNDATION THAT BUILT ITSELF

The family's charitable giving evolved organically through pooling resources for larger impact, as opposed to individual donations. When a local entrepreneur needed startup capital, the family provided both funding and mentorship.

"We discovered that giving together was more effective than giving separately," David's father observed. "And it taught the grandchildren that wealth comes with responsibility to help others."

THE SUCCESS THAT DIDN'T FEEL LIKE SUCCESS

"We didn't implement a dynasty blueprint," Michelle said during a recent family gathering. "We just started acting like we actually cared about each other's success instead of just assuming we did."

The transformation was gradual and organic. Their family learned how to approach their financial decisions through mutual support to make sure their success lasted for future generations.

WHAT ACTUALLY WORKS

THE THREE ELEMENTS THAT MATTER

After watching the Chen family's evolution, I've identified three elements that separate successful family wealth coordination from failed attempts:

Voluntary Participation: The moment family wealth coordination feels mandatory, it becomes toxic. Success requires genuine desire to help each other, not obligation.

Individual Autonomy: Coordination enhances individual success rather than controlling it. Family members maintain authority over their own decisions while gaining access to family wisdom and resources.

Organic Development: The most powerful systems are the ones that don't feel like systems. They emerge from family relationships rather than being imposed by frameworks.

THE QUESTIONS THAT GUIDE EVERYTHING

Instead of building elaborate governance structures, successful families can also focus on three simple questions:

1. **"How can we help each other succeed?"** This shifts the conversation from control to support.
2. **"What problems are we accidentally creating for each other?"** This identifies coordination opportunities without forcing them.
3. **"What do we want our family to be known for?"** This builds shared purpose without rigid rules.

THE ANTI-FRAMEWORK APPROACH

The Chen family succeeded because they avoided the trap of over-systematization. Although they did not build a formal dynasty blueprint, they learned how create a system by rebuilding their relationships with strong communication about financial decisions.

Their "system" consists of:

- Quarterly family calls to share what's happening in everyone's life and business
- Annual family gathering that combines vacation with light planning discussions

- Informal consultation before major decisions that might affect other family members
- Shared celebration of individual successes and mutual support during challenges

YOUR FAMILY'S NEXT STEP

THE ONE-HOUR CONVERSATION

You don't need a conference room at the Marriott or elaborate presentations. Start with a simple conversation:

"I've been thinking about how we can better support each other's financial goals. Would you be interested in talking about ways we might coordinate our planning without anyone losing control over their own decisions?"

THE THREE SIGNS YOU'RE READY

Family wealth coordination works when:

1. **Multiple family members have meaningful assets** to coordinate. It doesn't have to be millions! Just something substantial to get started.
2. **Family relationships are functional!** But remember, they don't have to be perfect.
3. **At least two people have to see potential benefits** in working together.

THE WARNING SIGNS TO AVOID

Don't attempt family wealth coordination if:

- Anyone is using it to control other family members
- Individual financial situations are chaotic or problematic
- Family relationships have unresolved conflicts that money discussions would inflame

THE REAL LEGACY

David's nightmare scenario of family members fighting over money instead of building it, became impossible because they'd chosen collaboration over competition.

But the deeper transformation was cultural. The Chen family developed what David calls "wealth generosity", which is the instinct to share opportunities rather than hoard them and to celebrate each other's success rather than compete with one another.

"My father came to America with nothing and built something," David reflected recently. "We took what he built and made it multiply not just financially, but relationally. That's the kind of legacy you can't put a dollar value on."

The most successful family wealth systems are the ones that make money secondary to relationships. When you get the relationships right, the money follows naturally.

Sometimes the most powerful dynasty is simply a family that chooses to build wealth together instead of alone.

CHAPTER 14

Why Not You? The Answer You've Been Waiting For

THE KITCHEN TABLE, FORTY YEARS LATER

I'm sitting at my own kitchen table now, reviewing client files on a Tuesday evening when Brooke walks in from lacrosse practice. She drops her gear by the door and grabs an apple from the counter, then notices the spreadsheets spread across the table.

"Dad, are you working on the Rodriguez family's college planning?"

I look up, struck by how casually she asked the question. At sixteen, Brooke knows my clients, understands their financial goals, and thinks strategically about wealth building like it's the most natural thing in the world.

"How did you know?" I ask.

"You mentioned they had twin daughters starting college next year. That spreadsheet looks like education funding projections."

As I watch her take a bite of apple and head upstairs to do homework, I'm transported back forty years to another kitchen table in Jersey City. A ten-year-old boy asking his mother why they always talked about stretching money instead of making more of it.

That boy couldn't have imagined this moment. He couldn't have envisioned a life where money conversations happen with confidence instead of anxiety, where wealth building is a family activity instead of a source of stress, and finally where the next generation learns abundance thinking as naturally as they learn to read.

The distance between that chipped Formica table and this solid oak one isn't measured in miles or years. It's measured in mindset shifts, mechanical systems, and the courage to believe that circumstances don't define destiny.

THE ANSWER WAS ALWAYS "NO REASON"

The question that started this journey—"Why not me?"—had a simple answer that took decades to understand: **There was never any reason it couldn't be you.**

Not your background, your education, your starting point, or your current circumstances. The only barriers between you and financial freedom are the stories you've accepted about what's possible for someone like you.

I learned this not through theory but through lived experience, client after client, family after family. The postal worker who built $1.7 million through systematic investing. The teacher who created a six-figure investment portfolio on a modest salary. The construction company owner who transformed chaos into coordinated wealth building.

None of them had special advantages. They had something more powerful: they refused to accept limitations as permanent.

THE THREE-PART TRANSFORMATION

This book took you through the same journey I traveled with my most successful clients. From scarcity to abundance, from survival to significance, and from managing money to building wealth.

PART I: MINDSET - "WHY NOT ME?"

Every financial transformation begins in your head. Until you change the story you tell yourself about money, no strategy or system will create lasting change.

The Martinez family lost nearly $1 million because they never shifted from scarcity thinking to abundance systems. They accumulated assets but never developed the mindset to preserve and transfer them.

Maria, the 26-year-old teacher, couldn't invest $200 monthly because she believed investing was for "other people." When we changed her identity from "non-investor" to "wealth builder," everything else became possible.

The mindset shift is this: Stop seeing yourself as a victim of circumstances and start seeing yourself as the architect of your financial future. The moment you take responsibility for your outcomes, you gain the power to change your life.

PART II: MECHANICS - "BUILDING THE BLUEPRINT"

Mindset without mechanics is just positive thinking. You need systematic approaches to cash flow, investing, and wealth architecture that work regardless of your emotions or external conditions.

The Four Seasons of Wealth taught you that your investment strategy should evolve with your life stage. Spring's aggressive growth allocation would destroy Winter retirees, just like Winter's conservative approach would limit Spring's wealth-building potential.

The Five Immutable Laws provided the framework that survives market cycles, economic changes, and emotional turbulence. You put to action that time trumps timing and discipline defeats brilliance. Diversification provides your only free lunch.

The mechanical truth is this: Wealth building isn't about finding perfect investments or timing markets. It's about implementing boring systems consistently over time while everyone else chases exciting strategies that fail.

PART III: LEGACY - "WHY NOT US?"

Individual wealth is just the beginning. True financial success extends beyond your lifetime to create generational impact.

The Chen family discovered that coordinating their wealth building multiplied everyone's success while strengthening family relationships. They proved that they didn't need rigid systems, instead needed shared commitment to each other's prosperity.

Brooke's financial education shows how preparing the next generation for wealth stewardship creates better outcomes than simply accumulating assets to transfer later. Capability development matters more than capital accumulation.

The legacy insight is this: The greatest inheritance isn't money; it's the wisdom, character, and systems that create money generation after generation.

THE STORIES THAT PROVE TRANSFORMATION IS POSSIBLE

Let me tell you about three clients who embody the complete journey from "Why not me?" to "Why not us?"

SARAH: FROM SURVIVAL TO SIGNIFICANCE

When I first met Sarah, she was a single mother earning $38,000 as a school administrator, convinced she'd never have enough money to matter. She lived paycheck to paycheck despite being brilliant with budgets and disciplined with spending.

"I'm good at making little money stretch," she told me, "but I'll never be someone who builds real wealth."

The Mindset Shift: We changed her identity from «good at being poor» to «wealth builder in training.» Instead of seeing her budgeting skills as survival tactics, we repositioned them as wealth-building foundations.

The Mechanical Implementation: Sarah started with $100 monthly into index funds. As her confidence grew, she increased contributions and eventually started a side consulting business helping other schools optimize their operations.

The Legacy Impact: Twelve years later, Sarah has now built a successful investment portfolio, owns rental properties, and runs a successful consulting practice. More importantly, her teenage daughter talks about money like Brooke does—strategically, confidently, abundantly.

"I used to think wealth was for other people," Sarah reflected recently. "Now I realize I was just other people who hadn't learned to think differently yet."

ROBERT: FROM CHAOS TO COORDINATION

Robert owned a successful construction company but felt like he was running on a financial treadmill. Despite earning substantial income, he never felt secure or wealthy.

"I make good money but never seem to get ahead," he confessed. "There's always something—equipment breaks, projects get delayed, taxes are higher than expected."

The Mindset Shift: Robert learned the difference between earning money and building wealth. His thinking evolved from «How do I make more?» to «How do I make what I earn work harder?»

The Mechanical Implementation: We implemented tax optimization strategies, systematic investing, and business structure improvements that redirected existing cash flow into wealth building without changing his lifestyle.

The Legacy Impact: Five years later, Robert has built substantial wealth while actually working less. His systematic approach freed up time for family and allowed him to start mentoring younger contractors in business management.

"I thought building wealth meant working more," Robert said. "Instead, it meant working smarter and letting systems do the heavy lifting."

THE MARTINEZ FAMILY: FROM CONFLICT TO COORDINATION

Remember Carlos Martinez, who died leaving his children to fight over a chaotic estate? His daughter Jennifer called me eighteen months later, determined to prevent similar chaos for her own family.

"We lost everything to lawyers and family fighting," Jennifer said. "I want to make sure my kids never go through what we did."

The Mindset Shift: The family moved from individual accumulation to coordinated planning. They started seeing themselves as a wealth-building team rather than competitors for limited resources.

The Mechanical Implementation: Jennifer and her siblings created coordinated estate plans, established family communication systems, and began building businesses together instead of separately.

The Legacy Impact: Three years later, the family has not only rebuilt what was lost but exceeded their father's success. They work together by choice, not obligation, and their children are learning financial literacy as a family activity.

"Dad tried to protect us by handling everything alone," Jennifer reflected. "We learned to protect each other by building everything together."

THE EXCUSES THAT KEEP PEOPLE TRAPPED

After working with hundreds of families, I've heard every reason people give for not building wealth. They all boil down to the same fundamental error that they believe their circumstances define possibilities.

"I DON'T EARN ENOUGH TO INVEST"

James built a seven-figure portfolio on a $65,000 salary. Maria created a six-figure portfolio earning $38,000. The amount you earn matters less than the percentage you invest and the time you give it to grow.

Truth: You don't need high income to build wealth. You need consistent investment of whatever income you have.

"I DON'T KNOW ENOUGH ABOUT INVESTING"

The most successful investors use the simplest strategies. Warren Buffett recommends index funds for most people. James' entire strategy was buying dividend stocks and never selling them.

Truth: Investment success comes from discipline, not intelligence. Simple strategies executed consistently beat complex strategies abandoned during difficulty.

"THE MARKET IS TOO RISKY RIGHT NOW"

There's never a perfect time to invest. People said markets were risky in 2009, which was actually the best buying opportunity in decades. Most believed it was risky to invest in 2016, and again in 2020.

Truth: The biggest risk is not participating in wealth building at all. Time in the market beats timing the market with mathematical certainty.

"I'M TOO OLD TO START"

A 50-year-old who starts investing has 15-20 years before retirement and potentially 30-40 years of life expectancy. That's plenty of time for compound growth to create meaningful wealth.

Truth: The best time to start was 20 years ago. The second-best time is now. Every day you delay will cost you potential growth.

"MY FAMILY DOESN'T UNDERSTAND MONEY"

Every family starts somewhere. The Chen family went from scattered individual efforts to coordinated wealth building in one conversation. The Martinez siblings rebuilt their relationships and their wealth after losing both.

Truth: Financial education can be learned at any age. Family financial cooperation can begin whenever someone has the courage to start the conversation.

YOUR MOMENT OF CHOICE

Right now, as you read these words, you may be facing the same crossroads I faced at that kitchen table thirty years ago.

You can continue accepting the financial limitations you've inherited, or you can start writing a different story.

You can keep managing scarcity, or you can start creating abundance.

You can remain a spectator to other people's success, or you can become the protagonist of your own financial transformation.

THIS MOMENT IS YOUR KITCHEN TABLE MOMENT.

The ten-year-old boy asking why his family always talked about stretching money instead of making more didn't know at the time that he was asking the most important question of his life. That question launched a journey that transformed not just his financial circumstances, but his entire understanding of what's possible.

Your question might be different:

- "Why do I always feel behind financially?"
- "Why can't I seem to get ahead no matter how hard I work?"
- "Why does wealth seem so impossible for someone like me?"
- "Why don't I know what my parents knew about money?"

But the answer is the same: **There's no reason you can't build the financial life you want except the limitations you've accepted as permanent.**

THE IMPLEMENTATION BLUEPRINT

Transformation happens through action, not intention. Here's your compass – a guide to change where you stand today and achieve the dreams that once felt impossible to reach.

Week 1: Mindset Foundation

- Write down your current money story, what you believe about wealth and who gets to have it
- Identify the financial identity you want to create
- Begin saying "I am a wealth builder" every morning until it feels true

Week 2: Mechanical Setup

- Open investment accounts and automate monthly contributions
- Calculate your wealth-building timeline using compound interest projections
- Implement the cash flow system that turns income into assets

Week 3: Seasonal Strategy

- Assess what wealth season you're in (Spring, Summer, Autumn, or Winter)
- Align your investment allocation with your life stage and timeline
- Create your seasonal transition plan for evolving strategy over time

Week 4: Legacy Planning

- Begin family conversations about values and financial coordination
- Complete basic estate planning documents appropriate for your situation
- Start preparing the next generation for financial responsibility

Month 2-12: System Optimization

- Refine your approach based on what you learn about yourself
- Increase investment amounts as your confidence grows
- Begin coordinating with family members who share your wealth-building commitment

Year 2+: Legacy Building

- Focus on developing others while continuing to grow your own wealth
- Create systems that outlast your individual involvement
- Build the family culture that sustains wealth across generations

YOUR SEASONAL ASSESSMENT: WHERE ARE YOU NOW?

Take this assessment to identify your current wealth season:

Age Factor:

- 20-35: Spring (+1 point)
- 35-50: Summer (+2 points)
- 50-65: Autumn (+3 points)
- 65+: Winter (+4 points)

Career Factor:

- Early career, growing income: Spring (+1)
- Peak earning years: Summer (+2)
- Pre-retirement planning: Autumn (+3)
- Retired: Winter (+4)

Responsibility Factor:

- Single, no dependents: Spring (+1)
- Married, young children: Summer (+2)
- Children approaching college: Autumn (+3)
- Empty nest, grandchildren: Winter (+4)

Risk Tolerance Factor:

- Can sleep through 40% portfolio drops: Spring (+1)
- Comfortable with 20-30% volatility: Summer (+2)
- Prefer 10-15% maximum swings: Autumn (+3)
- Need stable, predictable returns: Winter (+4)

Total Your Score:

- 4-6: Spring Season
- 7-10: Summer Season

- 11-14: Autumn Season
- 15-16: Winter Season

THE PORTFOLIO ALLOCATION MATRIX

Based on your seasonal assessment, here are the recommended portfolio allocations:

Spring Portfolio (Ages 20-35):

- 90% Stocks (60% U.S., 30% International)
- 10% Bonds
- Focus: Growth, accumulation, learning

Summer Portfolio (Ages 35-50):

- 80% Stocks (50% U.S., 30% International)
- 20% Bonds
- Focus: Optimization, tax efficiency, protection foundation

Autumn Portfolio (Ages 50-65):

- 60% stocks (40% U.S., 20% International)
- 40% Bonds/Cash
- Focus: Risk reduction, income planning, comprehensive legacy preparation

Winter Portfolio (Ages 65+):

- 50% Stocks (dividend-focused)
- 35% Bonds/Fixed Income

- 15% Cash/Money Market
- Focus: Income generation, capital preservation, legacy execution

YOUR FIVE LAWS IMPLEMENTATION CHECKLIST

Law #1 - Time

- Open investment account within 7 days
- Set up automatic monthly contributions
- Choose target date fund or simple three-fund portfolio

Law #2 - Discipline

- Write your investment policy statement
- Automate all investment contributions
- Commit to annual (not daily) portfolio reviews

Law #3 - Diversification

- Include bonds appropriate for your age
- Consider real estate and commodity exposure

Law #4 - Purpose

- Write down your specific financial goals
- Calculate how much you need to achieve them
- Connect investments to personal values and timeline

Law #5 – Protection

- Build emergency fund appropriate for your situation

- Review insurance coverage annually
- Update estate documents and beneficiaries
- Consider asset protection strategies

THE COMPOUND EFFECT OF COURAGE

Every transformation in this book started with someone who decided to stop accepting limitations as permanent. That decision creates a compound effect that extends far beyond individual financial circumstances.

When you change your relationship with money, you change what's possible for your children. When you build wealth systematically, you create opportunities for people you love. When you coordinate with family members, you multiply everyone's capacity for success.

But it starts with the courage to believe that your circumstances don't actually define your possibilities.

The difference between people who build wealth and people who don't isn't intelligence, luck, or starting point. It's the willingness to start before they feel ready and continue when others give up.

THE QUESTION THAT CHANGES EVERYTHING

Thirty years ago, a ten-year-old boy asked his mother a question that launched a journey from scarcity to abundance, from survival to significance, from managing money to building multigenerational wealth.

"Mom, why do we always talk about stretching what we have? Why don't we ever talk about how to make MORE?"

That question revealed something profound: **the limitations we accept are often self-imposed.**

Today, I ask you the question that has the power to transform your financial life:

WHY NOT YOU?

Why shouldn't you build the wealth that creates choices and opportunities for the people you love? Why shouldn't you design the financial life that reflects your values and supports your dreams? Why shouldn't you become the family member who changes the trajectory for generations?

There is no reason except the ones you've accepted as true.

But acceptance is optional. Limitations are negotiable. Stories can be rewritten.

The kitchen table where this journey began was marked by scarcity, anxiety, and the suffocating weight of financial limitation. The kitchen table where this story ends is marked by abundance, confidence, and the expanding possibilities that come from building wealth systematically.

Your financial transformation is waiting. Your family's legacy is waiting to be built. The only question remaining is the one that started it all:

Why not you? Why not now? Why not today?

The answer has been waiting for you all along: There's no reason you can't except the limitations you choose to accept.

Stop accepting them.

Start building.

Your wealth journey begins with your next decision.

Make it count.

IMPORTANT DISCLOSURES AND LEGAL NOTICES

Investment Advisory Services Disclosure

Manuel Ruiz, CFP® is the founder and managing partner of Compass Private Wealth, a registered investment adviser (RIA) with the Securities and Exchange Commission. This book is provided for educational and informational purposes only and does not constitute investment advice, financial planning advice, or a recommendation to buy or sell any specific securities.

Registration Notice: Registration as an investment adviser does not imply any level of skill or training. All investment advisory services are provided through Compass Private Wealth.

No Investment Advice: The content in this book should not be construed as personalized investment advice. All investment strategies and investments involve risk of loss, including the potential loss of principal. Past performance does not guarantee future results.

Consult Professionals: Before implementing any financial strategy discussed in this book, readers should consult with qualified financial, tax, and legal professionals who can provide advice tailored to their specific circumstances.

GENERAL DISCLAIMERS

Educational Purpose: This book is intended for educational purposes only. The strategies, concepts, and ideas presented are general in nature and may not be appropriate for all individuals or situations.

No Guarantee of Results: While the author has made every effort to provide accurate and reliable information, no guarantee is made regarding the accuracy, completeness, or results that may be obtained from using this information. Individual results will vary. "Hypothetical or Composite Performance: Examples in this book are composites or hypotheticals based on actual experiences but modified. Hypothetical performance is presented with assumptions [list if specific, e.g., 8% annual return] and risks; it may not reflect actual results for any investor."

Risk Disclosure: All investments carry risk, including the potential for loss of principal. Market volatility, economic conditions, inflation, and other factors can negatively impact investment performance.

Tax and Legal Considerations: Tax and legal implications of financial strategies can vary significantly based on individual circumstances and are subject to change due to legislative and regulatory developments. Always consult qualified tax and legal professionals.

PRIVACY PROTECTION NOTICE

Client Confidentiality: All client names, personal details, and specific circumstances described in this book have been altered to protect privacy and maintain confidentiality.

Composite Examples: Many examples represent composite scenarios drawn from multiple client experiences rather than single individual situations. While based on real circumstances, details have been modified, combined, or fictionalized to illustrate key concepts while protecting client privacy.

Family Stories: References to the author's family members, including his daughter «Brooke,» may include composite details or modified circumstances for privacy protection and illustrative purposes.

PROFESSIONAL STANDARDS

CFP® Certification: Manuel Ruiz holds the CERTIFIED FINANCIAL PLANNER® certification. CFP® professionals are held to fiduciary standards when providing financial planning services.

Continuing Education: The author maintains required continuing education and stays current with industry developments, regulatory changes, and best practices in financial planning and investment management.

IMPORTANT LIMITATIONS

Not Personalized Advice: This book cannot take into account your specific financial situation, investment objectives, risk tolerance, or other personal factors that are essential for making appropriate financial decisions.

Seek Current Information: Financial markets, tax laws, and regulations change frequently. Readers should verify current rules and regulations before implementing any strategies discussed in this book.

Professional Guidance: The complexity of financial planning often requires professional assistance. Consider working with qualified financial advisors, tax professionals, and estate planning attorneys.

CONTACT INFORMATION

For information about Compass Private Wealth's investment advisory services:

- Website: www.compasspw.com
- Phone: 908.615.2251
- Address: 51 JFK Parkway, Floor 1 West Ste 107, Short Hills, NJ 07078

Form ADV: Compass Private Wealth's Form ADV Part 2 brochure is available upon request and contains important information about the firm's services, fees, and business practices.

The author may receive compensation from the sale of this book. This book may contain references to third-party resources, websites, or services. The author does not endorse and is not responsible for the content or accuracy of third-party resources.

Last Updated: September 2025

This disclosure statement is subject to change without notice. Readers are encouraged to verify current regulatory requirements and firm disclosures before making financial decisions based on information in this book.

ABOUT THE AUTHOR

Manuel Ruiz, CFP®, is the financial advisor who cracked the code on why 70% of wealthy families lose their money by the second generation—and developed the proven strategies to prevent it. From Jersey City streets to Wall Street success, Manuel's transformation story embodies the journey from scarcity to abundance that he now guides others through daily. Growing up just one mile from Manhattan's financial district but worlds away from that wealth, Manuel learned from his Puerto Rican immigrant father that success is not about where you start, but how you think about what is possible. His father, an entrepreneur who named all three of his sons Hector, built a real estate empire through creative financing, tire shops, and sheer determination. His work planted the seeds of wealth psychology that would later revolutionize Manuel's approach to financial planning. As a CERTIFIED FINANCIAL PLANNER® professional with over 20 years of experience, Manuel has worked at prestigious Wall Street firms including JP Morgan, Merrill Lynch, Ernst & Young, and Prudential, where he discovered that traditional financial advice fails because it ignores human psychology. This revelation led him to develop his signature methodologies: "Four Seasons of Wealth" portfolio approach that aligns investment strategy with life stages, and the "Why Not Now? Why Not Me?" framework that transforms limiting beliefs into lasting financial freedom. Manuel has guided hundreds of families through major financial transitions, helping them build portfolios that align with both their financial goals and psychological comfort zones. His behavioral finance expertise has prevented countless families from making the emotional mistakes that typically destroy wealth across generations. As founder of Compass Private Wealth, Manuel specializes in multi-generational wealth planning and the psychology of money. His innovative approaches have made him a sought-after speaker at financial conferences and a trusted voice for families seeking to break generational financial patterns. Author of *Why Not Me?—Transform Your Thoughts, Take Control of Your Finances, and Unlock Lifelong Freedom,* Manuel bridges Wall Street sophistication with Main Street accessibility, making wealth building feel achievable as opposed to impossible. He lives in New Jersey with his wife Paola and daughter Brooke, whom he has taught that true wealth is not measured by what you have, but by what you enable others to achieve.